The Joyful Leader In You

*8 Secret Steps To Create Confidence
and Success In Life And Business*

The Award-winning Leader & Entrepreneur.

Kristy Guo

The Joyful Leader In You by Kristy Guo – Cuilan Guo. Foreword by Kristy Guo -Cuilan Guo First Edition 2023 Copyright © 2023Publisher **Signature Global Network PTY LTD.** All rights reserved.

No part of this publication may be reproduced, stored in a retrieval system, or transmitted in any form or by any means, electronic, mechanical, photocopying, recording, or otherwise, without the prior written permission from both the copyright owner and publisher. Disclaimer All the information, techniques, skills, and concepts contained within this publication are of the nature of general comment only and are not in any way recommended as individual advice. The intent is to offer a variety of information to provide a wider range of choices now and in the future, recognizing that we all have widely diverse circumstances and viewpoints.

Should any reader choose to make use of the information contained herein, this is their decision and the author and publishers do not assume any responsibilities whatsoever under any condition or circumstances.

ISBN: number 978-0-6456617-0-5 (Paperback)

For more information about the author, Kristy Guo, or for additional training, speaking engagements, or media inquiries, please visit: www.signaturegln.com

"To be the most attractive person is to own ability to unlock the joyful leader in you. Once you find the key to leadership of self-control, self-discipline, passion, purpose, peace, and love, nothing can shake, break, or destroy your identity and joy despite any up or down moments.

Everybody has unique gifts, and everyone deserves a fully joyful life. Find unique talents and make a difference by lighting up your inner leadership power. To be the light and be the delight will bring you unstoppable energy and joy.

I could hide my stories, but I choose to share them with you because I know that our life is not just about ourselves; it's much bigger than that!

Let's unlock your unstoppable and joyful leadership power to lead the best life; it will be a life-changing moment.

We only have this life once. Don't waste it!"

Kristy Guo (Cuilan)

Contents

Foreword — vii

Chapter One: Skim Milk, please! – Lead to make wise decisions, not excuses. — 1

Chapter Two: The beauty in you. – Lead to love and understand. — 25

Chapter Three: Joyful Leadership Myth. – Lead not to be offended. — 42

Chapter Four: Clear joyful leadership barrier. – Lead to let it go. — 78

Chapter Five: Joyful leading Faith. – Lead to Turn off your false alarm mechanisms. — 99

Chapter Six: Joyful Leadership Language. – Lead to speak powerfully. — 141

Chapter Seven: Joyful Leadership Power. – Lead to finish strong. — 158

Chapter Eight: Joyful self-motivated leadership. – Lead your best life. — 173

Bonus Powerful Quotes — 199
It's time to celebrate! — 205

Foreword

What is authentic leadership? Someone says it is a responsibility; someone says it is an example; someone says it is a sacrifice; someone says it is love; someone says it is parenting. Leadership is more highlighted nowadays, but something is missing, and that is joy.

You probably heard of many excellent books, and leadership articles, such as <Start with why> by Simon Sinek, <Good to great>by Jim Collins, etc., but are they aligned with your life? They were more regarding leadership in the business or a team rather than life. After all, work is only a tiny part of our life. Our life is much bigger than just working. Finding a joyful leader in you is not just in your workplace but more in your life.

Hi, I am Kristy. I was born in a small town, grew up with a tough childhood, and suffered many physical and mental health struggles. However, despite all the unfortunate experiences in my youth, I became a fearless and confident entrepreneur and an author — a happy wife with a happy marriage and two blessed children.

With twenty years of corporate world working experience, I travelled to about 15 countries and 30+ cities worldwide before I was 27, and I have been consistently in leadership roles. Received work sponsorship twice and had work experience in some top worldwide logistics companies.

I have humbly won some awards since school and my working career. However, my passion is not winning awards; it is about making a difference in people's lives and helping more people.

In 2021, I officially became an author and an audiobook speaker. In Jan. 2022, I formally became an entrepreneur by launching my business, SGN -Signature Global Network PTY LTD, a global logistics network. From the day I started my business, not a year, our company has achieved 80+ global member offices in our network. I got thousands of professional logistic connections up to today. My company SGN and I recently received a multicultural business award from a local AU Mumpreneur (Australian Mum entrepreneur) and a few other awards nominations. In 2022, I was featured on a magazine cover and in various global media channels, such as the USA, Asia, and Europe. Was a speaker at multiple events, such as the logistics TV channel and the women in the supply chain.

Most importantly, I saw people transforming their lives and the positive impact I could make on people's lives. My passion is always about helping people achieve joyful leadership in life and career.

Ok, enough about me. This book is not about me but you. First, thank you for choosing my book. Well done! Because you have already been qualified as one of the elements a true leader has, which is that a true leader remains hungry, humble, and never stops learning. They learn from anywhere and anytime. I am thrilled to disclose all my life experiences and helpful tools that helped me to reach where I am today. I've become a truly fearless leader and confident dream achiever of my own life. The methodologies I used will help you transform your life as well.

Are you too busy to even sit down and read a book? Are you too busy to find out what's happening with you and your purpose? Are you struggling with self-empowerment? Are you wondering if you are born as a leader and if not, how can you lead? Are you thinking, how on earth could I be happy with so many uncertainties in life? How could I be joyful with so many bad things or challenges happening in my life? Have you ever got a moment like saying to yourself that: "Life is too hard," or a moment you say to yourself: "I don't have a choice."

The Joyful Leader In You

There are so many books, authors, suggestions, ideas, and information you receive and know every day, but why is there no fixed formula to 'success' 'never get angry', or 'never get upset'? 'Remain confident forever' 'Never be offended? We are all unique individuals. Can we find a way to solve all issues? We can't because there are always new problems and situations. However, if we could find and understand these two words in our life that can potentially be answers to all our issues, our life would function much better. Therefore, we can enjoy every moment, despite our circumstances or situations. The answer is to find your **Purpose** and **Faith**.

Everyone can enjoy their life and live it to the most and be their best version if they can focus on their 'purpose' and 'faith.' Purpose drives your life direction. Faith keeps you going and keeps you away from fear. Imagine your life is full of intentions, goals, dreams, meaningful tasks, Confidence, Hope, Fearlessness, and Trust. You will never give up, and you will be full of joy. Purpose gives birth to faith, and faith drives more purpose into you.

We can know and understand many things, but we may not know how to abide by them in life. The frustrating part is even though we used what we knew, it seems nothing could last forever. For example, you had a 100% perfect day, but then the next day, things all went wrong; You had a massive group of fans who love and respect you, but then you meet someone who is entirely impolite and disrespectful to you. You ticked one thing from your bucket list, but you still felt something was missing, and it wasn't as exciting as you expected. You are always confident, but you are facing a new situation this time, and fear starts to attack your mind. You use the same strategy you used that was always successful in dealing with a new person in life, but the result turned out to be completely different. Maybe it is anything else that you have always been very confident about, but you made a big mistake, so you started to doubt if you are good at it. Why? How can good things last longer, then?

The good news is that you can find the most answers through this book, find your unique way of self-help, and unlock your inner leadership power with your passion for finding your 'Purposes,' 'Faith,' and ability to 'Love' and 'lead.'

The bad news is that if you know what to do, but you still choose not to do it or keep going the 'comfortable old way,' or if you don't even have the patience to finish reading this book, then I highly doubt that you shall get the most from it. That's why with the same book and learning, someone takes away 100%. Someone takes only 1% or nothing. After reading, they put it aside and feel like watching another Netflix or Disney movie, and then they keep doing their old way and old life. No sugar-coating, but if you have bought this book, you also should have committed to gaining the most value from it and applying the helpful tips in your life, my friend! Now it is your choice if you want to take 1% or up to 100%.

Looking at the current world, honestly, why do you need to pay so much money to join hundreds of different coaching or programs when you already have the inner power you need to unlock and light it up? My passion is to help every one of you to be the best version of yourself. You need to use this book as a key to open the door to access the authentic YOU with unstoppable leadership power and everlasting happiness in life.

You must be determined and committed if you pay any money for a program, coaching, seminar, or summit to learn. Without commitment and consistency, it is ultimately a waste of your time.

If you focus on doing something and believe you can do it, then you DECIDED to do it, it will always be successful with your determination as long as you NEVER GIVE UP. The game is never over until you say it is. Don't stop the game! Just enjoy it!

Give yourself time. It is like this book; I want you to enjoy it, and apply the methodology to your life. Give yourself time to know yourself better and grow to be better every day! Our life is a journey, not a destination!

Promise me you will finish reading and apply the secret tips in your life. In that case, I promise you that you will unleash your joyful leadership in all areas of your life!

Share your stories with me, and I would love to hear from you by contacting me through our supporting email: sgninfo@signaturegln.com or any of my social channels.

LinkedIn: https://www.linkedin.com/in/cuilan-kristy-guo-1776b5182
Instagram: Kristy_guochangemaker
Facebook public main page: https://www.facebook.com/kristyguochangemaker/
Twitter: @Cuilanguo

Happy reading!!

CHAPTER ONE

Skim Milk, please!

Lead to make wise decisions, not excuses.

My kids got full quickly when I cooked something they didn't like; I asked them if they wanted more, and the answer was NO. But in a few minutes, they could eat another ice cream, a cake, a bowl of yogurt, a box of crackers, and whole plates of fruits right after dinner.

One of my family relatives always has her diet moments, and once we asked her to eat a bit more food (a relatively healthy one) but she said she was on a diet that month, but the next day when we went out for dinner, she could eat so many fried foods that have much more calories and are more junk.

A guy in the USA did a series of videos called the Gold-Digger Prank, which recorded those moments when he pretended to make friends with some hot girls who would immediately reject him in the first place. But when they saw his luxurious and expensive car, they changed their minds and immediately wanted to be friends. This group of people is called as gold-diggers, the meaning of a gold-digger is: *a person whose romantic pursuit of, relationship with, or marriage to a wealthy person is primarily or solely motivated by a desire for money.* Yes, sadly, they are, and sadly so many people nowadays have a wrong purpose in life and are obsessed with money and power, right?

My point is about the choice that we make. All of these stories can always go with different endings if they make another choice. I am going to share with you some of my true stories, and you will find yourself in some of the stories, but most importantly, you will then find your unique way to become a leader who makes wise choices in life rather than excuses.

It was a very early morning, probably 4 or 5 am. I was going on a business trip across the USA and Latin America with the company CEO and two other colleagues. We were sitting at the airport café. After a ton of check-ins, check-outs, security checks, and waking up in the morning after so many days of traveling and tight scheduled meetings, everyone looked tired. It was the best time to have a brief rest before we had to board the plane again.

We were sitting in a fancy bar with various kinds of drinks.

'What would you like to drink, please?' the waitress asked with an extreme American accent.

'Coke Zero,' our CEO responded.

'Latte, please! Lemon tea for me!" the other two colleagues said.

My turn again, and this time, I did not hesitate, and with a confident smile, I said: "Skim milk, please!" As expected, the waitress was shocked and tried to clarify: "Excuse me, I beg your pardon?"

I smiled at all the others' judgment and waves of laughter, and I confirmed: "Yes, I want a glass of skim milk, please!"

The waitress said: "OK then." Her face was still bemused as she spoke to the other two servers, who laughed out loud. However, their reactions didn't bother me anymore.

It wasn't always the case. People didn't realize that it was probably the tenth time I was asked what I wanted to drink, but the first time I hadn't struggled to say what I truly wanted. And the first time I felt relief. Previously, when other waiters and my boss laughed at me, I would doubt myself, and my first instinct would be: am I normal? Am I weird? Or am I just immature?

But something had changed. I felt **so good** that day. Before that, I was struggling to think how not to make myself look like an idiot or a potential laughingstock to people. I would try to accommodate others to order something that I didn't want but might make me look better. Because I thought only to be the same or similar to them make myself look good. I tried coffee, which made me uncomfortable, as I could not handle the caffeine. I tried tea, then I couldn't sleep, and I tried juice, but I knew they have high sugar, and I always wanted to be sugar-free as I knew the harm sugar could bring me. Skim milk was the choice that represented me the most back then. Yes, I just wanted to have the courage to be myself.

I always said yes when people asked me to eat what they liked, but I didn't. Like the junk food I knew would make me fat and unhealthy, I did not say no, just because I cared too much about how others were thinking. I didn't know how to say no because I was fearful that my choice wasn't right or that it might offend someone.

That reminded me of when I was always one of the youngest in the class and the workplace. I wasn't confident at all. I'd instead follow others to play safe than make a wrong choice. I was super fearful of being judged by others. I was utterly letting others lead my life.

But I finally lived a healthy lifestyle in the last few years; I never wanted junk going into my body again, and I did not want to go back to where I was. The unconfident girl could not fit into the beautiful dress that she wanted. It wasn't frustrating, upset and lost. I spent a tough year trying to lose weight, and finally, I made it. But I still cared too much about how others looked at me. I lost track of what I needed and what was good for me.

What's worse, I would also try to explain to people to let them understand, and if they didn't, I would be embarrassed and then start to doubt myself again. Am I normal? Am I weird? Will they understand me? That will make me look so bad....

But wait, why do I have to do that? I don't have to. When I realized that my decision could transform my life and that I am the decision-maker for my own life. I realized that I should have taken the lead in my life. Others cannot make decisions for me unless I give them permission.

Is this familiar to you? Do YOU care too much about how others look at you? Do you always try to explain to people that you are worried about what they think of you?

The day I said: 'Skim Milk Please,' with a relaxed smile, I realized: **You always have a choice! Will you choose what's right for you? Others' advice is good, but you don't need their approval to choose something that is best for you.** That has been one of the most significant decisions in my life! Why? Because I found it is always your choice whether you let people lead you or you lead yourself.

You are the authentic leader of your life. Sometimes you may feel that you do not have a choice, then you start to change from being proactive to reactive, and you give your choice to others. Then, you will always be disappointed because nobody knows you better than yourself.

Even today, I still order milk or even baby chino instead of coffee. If my choice offends anyone who loves or thinks coffee is the best, it's their choice, not mine. I cannot judge their choices either. I have no authority in others' life choices. It is the same if you choose to be a vegetarian, a meat-lover, a truck driver, a bus driver, a cleaner, a director, a producer, a cosplayer, a game designer, or any identity you want to be. Maybe it is your dream job, but you are worried about people's opinions. Will you let others decide your dream for you?

The first time I felt others judging me for my age and gender was when I was 18-year-old and I was at a logistics network global conference in Guangzhou, China. "Are you from high school or college?" "What are you doing here?", they'd laugh.

Being a young female manager, I was looked down upon. It made me very insecure; I dressed in older styles to make myself look more mature.

Once I ordered that skim milk, I realized that my identity isn't based on what others say about me, but on how I think of myself.

You will always hear noises from people around you. Because we humans always want to control others, we forget we are the best leaders of ourselves, not others. Leaders are supposed to impact and influence, not force others to do what they want.

We, humans, must learn to respect each other's choices and not take offense. Therefore, when people disagree with you, you do not have to feel judged. Be courageous and choose what is best for you. **Order your own 'skim milk'** and shut down any noises.

When is your 'skim milk' moment? A moment when you know clearly what you want and why you want it. A moment that you are leading yourself, not letting others lead your choices. A moment you are courageous to be your authentic self.

Find your SKIM MILK moment and keep it! Because you are not supposed to be **the same** as everyone else! You are supposed to be extraordinary, not ordinary. It is one of the most precious things that you could defend. Be 'YOU!'

You always have a choice! It is your decision. What you decide leads to what is going to happen! When I was afraid to order my skim milk. It felt like I did not have a choice because of the fear of being judged. In our life, whenever we make a choice that we regret later, the most common words we say are: "I don't have a choice!" Is it true?

This is becoming a common excuse for people. Many people say:

"We are the products of our environment." This is partly true because each new generation varies from the way how they were raised and the environment during the new time. But let's be honest, it is never *the environment* that chose for us. We are the **final decision-makers. We** are responsible for **our choices.** *The environment is not a person who can make her own decisions, in fact, it is changed by people.*

It reminds me of the situation when I once saw a little boy fall to the ground; the next moment, his grandma came and hit the ground, trying to comfort the boy by saying: "Bad floor." That shocked and irritated me. Why? She wasn't helping the boy to become strong and responsible; she was unconsciously ruining his future, just because she wanted him to feel better in the short run.

When my daughters fell or got hurt because of their careless behaviours, I always asked them to say sorry, because they should have been more careful about looking after themselves and the things around them. That helped them to take responsibility and be more careful in the future.

The other common words we say often is: "I can't do it because the environment didn't allow me to." This becomes the easiest way for us to set all the limitations and excuses to what we could achieve in life. But is that entirely true? Remember the 'skim milk' moment for me? I felt like I did not have a choice. I had to pick something I didn't like, just to please others and look better. Was I forced by a gun to my forehead to stop me from ordering the skim milk? No, my fear controlled me. To be a joyful leader, one of the most important tasks we need to do is to be aware of the unwise choices we make every day, and turn them into wise ones.

Can we agree on this? Don't say, "I don't have a choice!" Don't make others responsible for your choices. Yes, **you may have limited choices, sometimes too limited**, but you still have the option to choose. It is like I felt my colleagues forced me to order other drinks or that the environment forced me to make that choice, but none of this is true. **We own our will and responsibility.** Don't assume that others or the environment are forcing your choices. **You are the one who sets your own boundaries.**

You may ask: "What about when we face tragedies, illness, or physical limitations?" You are right, when bad things and unfortunate things happened in life without our control, *we cannot change the situation*, but *we can always choose how we will respond.*

Have a look at the explanation of 'excuse' in the Oxford dictionary:

Excuse Verb, 1, seek to lessen the blame attaching to (a fault or offence); try to justify: 2, release (someone) from a duty or requirement: Noun, 1, a reason or explanation given to justify a fault or offence:

We must be cautious not to get into the trap of choosing an excuse. Nobody can control your brain to select for you unless you release yourself from the duty of making that choice.

We do have choices, but regarding making choices, one of the most sensitive and essential things is 'Freedom'. We always ask ourselves: "Do I have the freedom to make that choice?" or "Why can't I have freedom to do whatever I want?" Ok, can I ask you a question: "Does having a choice really make us happy?"

I love this article *Posted by: Kate Torgovnick May* **July 18, 2012 at 3:00 pm EDT With its title:** Does having choice make us happy? 6 studies suggest it doesn't always. Check the full story on this link: https://blog.ted.com/does-having-choice-make-us-happy-6-studies-that-suggest-it-doesnt-always/

Here are some of the contents it says: "In a fascinating talk at TEDxStanford, "Sometimes it's good to give up the driver's seat," "The most harrowing and agonizing part of the whole experience was that we were making decision after decision," Shiv shares in his talk. "The wisdom of the ages is that when it comes to decisions of importance, it's best to be in charge. But are there contexts where we're far better off taking the passenger seat and having someone else drive?"

"Shiv decided to test the theory on undergraduate students about to solve word puzzles. While one set of students was asked to choose between two teas — caffeinated or relaxing chamomile — the other group was told by the researchers which of the teas to drink. In the end, the students assigned a tea solved more puzzles than those who were given a choice. Shiv hypothesized that this is because making the choice allows a person to have doubt about their decision when faced with the prospect of immediate feedback."

"Shiv's thoughts on choice are counterintuitive. But his work is part of a growing body of research on choice."

What is **freedom**? First, let me share some stories about myself when I was younger. This will help you to understand more about *freedom* along the way.

I was born in a small town, and my parents were always too busy earning money to support the family. That was the old days when most families were more focused on fighting to get milk and butter for their families, rather than where they could go for holidays or parties like nowadays. Complete different time.

I rarely got the proper care and attention from them because they were not always around. The only good thing about that was my freedom to do what I wanted. However, sometimes, I'd need to find ways to feed myself. Sometimes, to survive by myself, I intentionally sat in front of a neighbour's house to get their attention and waited for them to invite me for dinner. Physically, I was free and could go anywhere, even though I was only seven years old. However, spiritually, not just because I felt lonely and left behind, but also because the domestic violence often happened in front of me back then. My father got an alcohol problem and always hits my mum. I constantly felt emotionally trapped.

Crying became one of the easiest ways to let my emotions out. I was very sensitive and easily angered. I felt lonely, insecure, and full of fear. I felt stuck and wished I could choose a different family. Like many girls,

I wished I could live in a fairy tale, a princess to be taken care of while doing the things I loved.

Physically, I was free to go anywhere I wanted because my parents didn't have time to care for me. But I didn't feel free because I struggled for their love and attention. Mentally I was stuck on the same treadmill: "Why is it always me? Why do I have to be a grown-up when I am just a child? Where is my childhood? Why can't I just have a normal family? Where is my mum? Where is my dad? Who can I rely on to help me? What future do I have? Does anyone even care about me? Who am I?"

And the most distractive and distressing thought: "Why do others get to have a happy family?" Yes, I compared myself with others, just like most of us do. And that was the biggest mistake of all.

We all value freedom, whether we are religious or not. As I've matured, I've now seen that freedom is a **fear-free and free choice**. It's the freedom to find inner peace. Everything follows perfectly from that peaceful mind.

For example, when masks were mandatory during the COVID pandemic, there were people who didn't want to wear them; they felt that their freedom was robbed. How about students? Not everyone wants to go to school, but they still need to. Does it mean that their freedom is robbed? True freedom is not to do whatever you want, but to choose how you respond. Let's be honest, there is no absolute freedom.

You may say: "I just want to be free to do whatever I want. Are you trying to stop me?" I believe that is everyone's dream – **Get whatever you want and live a worry-free life.** Because we all think if we get whatever we want, then we shall be completely happy. Everybody wants to do what they want with no restrictions. That includes me. When I was younger, I was defensive; I was unhappy when things didn't go my way or when people didn't do what I said.

OK, let's imagine you are the only person left on the earth. Yes, you can do whatever you want without overthinking the consequence. Even if there is a consequence, you will be the only one affected, and then you will learn and grow from the lesson. What you are doing won't affect anybody else but you. You can also set up all the rules and do whatever you like. But I don't believe you will be happy.

Everything has two sides to reflect on other side. If there is only one side, there's no way to reflect on the other side. If you never feel hate, you shall never know what love is. If you never know bad things, you shall never know what good things mean.

If you truly want to be free, you must understand and embrace the fact that you are not the only person on earth. There was a TV series called The Last Man On Earth. In the story, there was the last man on earth who enjoyed all the resources, had, and did everything he wanted. He was happy for a short while. Then he realized that life wasn't about how good he felt, how satisfied he was when he got whatever he wanted. It was also not about how much physical freedom he had. It was about getting inner peace and joy. Without these, whether he did or went wherever he wanted, he still felt trapped and remained unhappy. Until the day he realized true freedom is to control how you respond. To be calm and stable from the deep inside of you.

Emotions constantly controlled me when I was a child. I was about 8 when I thought of leaving my family. I was so angry and disappointed at my unfair situation- not feeling loved, the neglect, and the family violence. The more I suffered, the more I wanted freedom. In my mind, to be free was to run away from my situation. Back then, I thought escaping from reality would free me from the pain.

But I was wrong. How many times can we run away from our situations? Are we going to hide and avoid pain for our whole life?

When the pain grew too much, I had to choose to stay where I was and keep suffering or to control how I respond. That's when I realized that I was not the only one on earth. The decision opened my eyes to see others who were worse off. Such as hungry homeless people, orphans, young beggars, and thieves. I realized my life wasn't that bad compared to many. Because we are free, we can choose which way to go. Positive or negative. I chose to be positive and see things with gratitude.

Freedom is not about getting whatever you want! It is about freeing yourself from being controlled by your emotions and responding positively to any situation, even if it doesn't work out as you wish. Your freedom – the free choice is to choose to lead with self-control and determination and make wise decisions in everything you do.

Making a decision that is free from emotion isn't easy, but it can be easier if we take the lead and are willing to take responsibility.

If we google 'how many decisions we as humans are making in a day, the answer will come up with 35,000 for each of us. That is a shocking and fascinating number, isn't it? If we turn right or left, where are we going next? Should we go to the bathroom or not? Should we eat now or later? Which clothes are we going to wear today? Which colour should we pick? How much water do I need to drink today? Should I be hard or soft when talking to my children about the mistake they just made? This list can go on forever. How amazing are we? How awesome you have been making decisions every day! You are an expert!

We have many choices to make, but when we choose to be negative, we immediately feel there's no choice. That leads to a path of low motivation, excuse-making, a victim mindset, lack of responsibility, and little self-control.

When we choose to be positive and not to be controlled by our emotions, we know we always have a choice. That leads to a path of self-motivation, problem-solving, self-determination, responsibility, and self-control.

Like the skim milk moment, making better decisions in life starts with **choosing a positive life attitude, leading our emotions, and being a proactive, courageous, and responsible leader.**

You may say: "It is so easy to say, but how do we make these decisions when life gets so hard?" You may say: "How could we ignore our emotions?"

Emotions are part of us, but we must train ourselves to lead and control emotions and not let them control us. In the other words, if you are feeling emotional, you cannot ignore them, you need to deal with them with your knowledge, experience, and mature responses. Emotions are good only if we are aware of them and choose not to make decisions when we consciously know it's a wrong timing.

There's no formula as to what **mature response** is. Do not chase perfect responses, because even mature leaders make mistakes too, but the point that makes a difference is that they always keep practicing, learning, and growing. Here are some of my stories that I had to make decisions in my life and I believe can reflect some of your own stories and help you to make better decisions from now on.

What decision will you make if you suffer domestic violence?

I suffered domestic violence in my family, as mentioned previously.

My father always got drunk and would hit my mum on her head, face and body. and I sometimes worried that my Mum could die because of the severe injuries.

It was heartbreaking. I was very fearful. I was very young and didn't know how to deal with the situation. I felt ashamed to share this secret with anyone at all. I love my parents, but I was suffering from so many emotions when I had to face so many new and complicated situations. I was unsure of what the next day would bring me. I had choices: one is to escape from my house, and hide as far as I can; two, I could find people to help me, but then my dad would be in trouble; and three, I could try to stop the violence.

So, I chose option three, I was scared but I had to try to stop those situations. My Dad would never hit me though, so my help did stop some of the tragedies. However, it only worked for a short time, then it would happen again. I remember there were times when the three of us sat together for dinner, my Dad started to complain about how tasteless the dish was, then when my mum wanted to explain, my Dad already had thrown the bowls on the floor and started to hit my mum. I would then scream and cry loudly. It repeated so many times.

What could I do next? I couldn't change the situation, as I tried, so I had to find ways to help myself. Then I found one of the self-healing processes is to write journals. I decided to find a peaceful place where I could tell all my secrets safely. So that I could move on in my life. I decided to be my best friend. I comforted myself during the writing process.

It was one of the most magical experiences that unlocked so much positivity within me. It brought me hope and joy, and every time after crying and writing my diaries, I felt relief. Through the diary, I found a self-comfort voice that was telling me: "There must be something your Dad was going through and suffering too, even though you don't know what it is." Also voices like: "Look at what makes you happy. Write down the positive things in your life." When I looked back, I started to understand more about why. The behavior was still unacceptable but at least the journal experience helped so much with my self-healing so that I could live without carrying so many negative emotions. That was a huge help for me to become a positive person, and no matter what happened, I could always hold a great attitude of positivity to live and to move on.

What decision will you make if someone bullies you?

I suffered from being bullied in my childhood, and one of the cases that hurt me the most was at primary school.

My hometown wasn't a well-developed city in China. When I studied, there weren't any anti-bullying protections in place. Unlike today's 'Zero tolerance.'

I remember there was a naughty classmate whose name was Tao. I was always the youngest in the class, and he always chose me to bully.

He was tall and strong but he behaved very abnormally compared to many other classmates. He annoyed me and said bad things to me sometimes. Laughed at me for no reason, and sometimes even took my chair away when I was about to sit down. Once, he cut one of my two ponytails super short when I was focusing on doing my own task. That day I cried like a baby, I was heartbroken because it took me so long to grow my hair back. Because of that, I had to cut the other side and regrow it. The teacher and the principal did little. That was the environment I was in and the time that bullying wasn't seriously treated by anybody. Thus, I was always living in fear and had to intentionally avoid the bully by myself.

But slowly, as I had to move on from the past pain and look at things differently, I realized that avoiding wasn't the best way to overcome my fear. Therefore, I rehearsed talking to him to get to know him and his problems. I tried to be nice to him, and I helped him with his study. Then I realized he had been facing significant issues in his family, and he couldn't control his emotions. He lost his self-control easily, maybe it is called some of the mental health illness nowadays, but it was defined 30+ years ago, especially where I lived- a small developing town.

I still had to stay away from him because his behaviours could be so aggressive. In fact, I wasn't the only one he bullied. I found that many other boys bullied him and made him hate people. He bullied a few other younger ones and he only found those who were less strong to hurt. After knowing that, I did not feel I was the victim anymore, and I tried to stop others from doing bad things to him, and I tried to help whenever I could from then on.

I felt much better after understanding the whole situation because I realized it wasn't about me. I wasn't the poor one. The boy was. That taught me: **When anyone does something bad to you, that person must have their own problems. Do something to help, if not, show sympathy and walk away.** This story could have had a worse ending if I had dwelled myself into a victim role, chosen to believe and feel sorry that I wasn't likable. That was why the boy decided to bully me. I am so glad that I had made a better decision.

What decision will you make if you suffer from horrible health conditions and have your life at risk?

I did suffer from bad health conditions. I was overweight because I found eating helped my anxiety. I found comfort in eating. That was when I didn't need to think much, just feed my body and enjoy that satisfaction. That caused my health to a bad condition.

I also had stomach problems, because of irregular eating habits. Some days, my parents would provide me with meals, but other days, nobody would come home and cook. I remember once after I finished my evening self-learning class at school, and I came home with an empty stomach. After feeling hungry for a while, I started sweating and had a severe cramping. I was on the floor for a long time until my mum came home and took me to the hospital. They told us I had hyperchlorhydria because I didn't eat properly or on time.

Besides that, I always got the flu and many strange illnesses when I was little. One of the biggest issues that I always had was whenever I got the flu, I would cough for at least three months. My Mum had tried western and eastern doctors with all the medicines or herbs that could potentially cure me, but it always ended up not working.

One of the biggest health issues which almost took my life away was the heat stroke I suffered in the summer. My body wasn't fit at all, especially being overweight. I remembered it was a school summer holiday after I played with my sister at her classmate's house. It was so hot, probably 40 degrees. The summer heat made me so sick, and while walking back home under the sun, I had to stop to rest a few times and felt like vomiting and was feeling short of breath. After my sister and I reached home, I couldn't hold the vomiting anymore, so I vomited for about a few minutes; right after, I fainted. My sister was laughing at me and thought I was pretending, later she realized something was wrong, and she then panicked and started to call mum to help.

If it wasn't a neighbour who did the first aid for me and got me back, I could have already gone. I still remember the day I could feel and vaguely see many people gathered around me to watch me while the hero neighbour was trying to save my life. That day taught me: **Love and enjoy your life every day because you won't know when your last day is.** And I was very grateful for those people who came and saved my life. I treated them as heroes deeply in my heart. That was also when I became more passionate about anyone, even strangers around me. They helped me to gain hope of **believing in people** again.

What's more, there were many times that I felt I was forgotten, and I thought it was because I wasn't excellent enough. There was once when I tried on the dress I loved, but it turned out to be a disaster, because I was too unfit.

There were so many times when I tried to get rid of the sugar but failed. There were so many times when I was trying too hard to raise people's attention but failed. There were so many times when I felt I had to do more to prove myself, but the more I tried, the less confident I became once I failed. There were so many times when I thought because of my imperfect family background, I was not worth being loved, and I was meant to live a secondary life. So many negative thoughts were constantly attacking my mind because of my suffered situations.

I kept living my life and most of the areas of my life was going well because of my positive attitude, but there's something missing and that is a true transformation inside out.

One day, a mean colleague laughed at me loudly in front of other people: "How could you be a manager if you couldn't even manage your own shape?" That hurt me badly and it became one of the life-turning points for me.

"Enough suffering!" I remember what I said to myself the day when I heard from the colleague. I cried for so long after going home, because of all the bitterness and burdens in me. *I decided to fight my battle and lead my way.* I started my losing weight journey seriously. I called the colleague a mean guy back then, but I appreciated him more afterward. He was right. I didn't feel the importance of managing my health. A better shape is not just for a better look but for better physical and mental health. This lesson taught me that sometimes, only strong words that possibly hurt you can wake you up, sugar-coding words keep you sleeping.

The losing-weight journey was very challenging. I had to get up early in the morning to do exercise, and there were many times that I almost gave up. It was very hard for me as it wasn't on my routine before, but the goal that I had about what I wanted and needed the change kept me going. I said to myself: "*I need a TRANSFORMATION, because I don't want to stay where I am, and suffer all these physical and mental health issues so often again! I have bigger dreams to achieve, but if I don't have good health, I cannot go further.*"

In order to achieve the quickest results in the shortest time, I searched for so many ways from books or resources about how to lose weight, and I then concluded my way to do it most effectively. I knew that because everyone's body, lifestyle, and circumstances are all so different, so I had to figure out a way that fit me the most.

The choice I made was that I had to get rid of any soft drinks, sugar, and carbohydrate. The wise decision I made was to avoid going out with people if there were food attractions. Whenever I was feeling hungry, I would talk to myself and say: "I am not hungry. I am just thirsty." Then I would have grabbed a glass of water to drink. I remember having only yogurt and wholegrain bread for dinner and eating nothing after 6 pm. Once I couldn't help putting some dessert into my mouth, but after chewing, I had to split it out. It was a bit disgusting, but it was the only effective way and it was a battle that I had to fight. I didn't give up, because I knew that only making a change would reduce the pain by remaining the same. To lose weight was just one small step to the leading of all other transformations. There were more things in my life that I knew I needed a change, but getting started was the first and the biggest step. Remember, every small step counts.

It was hard, I failed, then I got up trying again, failed again, but I tried again, again, and then again. As time went by, I found the strength to overcome my weakness. In the first month, I saw a bit of change in my body shape; In three months, my clothes got looser; In six months, the sizes I wore went smaller. In one year, I could wear size M and then S. The transformational journey made me energetic and joyful every day. It's not just my physical health got improved, but also my mental health. I found the cheerful leader in me that is taking the lead in making wise choices and enjoying the slight but continuous improvement with each effort made.

Through the journey, I also practiced a great habit of commitment. If I decided to be committed to anything, I would do it with determination. Not 80%, not 90%, not 99.9%, always 100%. It always worked with my strong will. That was why I was so determined at the Skim Milk moment and **never wanted to go back again.**

What decisions will you make in your life now? What would you do if you faced a similar situation as mine? What areas in your life do you feel you needed a change, but you couldn't and then gave up? It's frustrating that many people always do the wrong things but expect the right results. If you want to lose weight, you should get rid of soft drinks, do some diet, and monitor what you eat; If you want to be healthy, then quit smoking and stop eating junk; If you want to have a better body shape, then commit to exercise regularly. Nowadays many people eat lots of fast food such as MacDonald, KFC, and instant noodles, and they are suffering from health issues, but they are expecting for a doctor's appointment or medicines to solve their problems. Are you like that? I used to. I used to eat more than 100% full, eat deserts, and expect magic to lose weight. I used to sleep late and irregularly but expected to have good health. Until I found my joyful leader in me. The leader who helped me to make wise decisions in life that brings me peace and alignment.

When my daughter was doing a workout with me for the first time, and her tummy hurt so much, then she would try to find an easier way to do it instead. I couldn't help but telling her: "So are you expecting to have a nap and a massage in the GYM room? You are here to work out for a better result, then why do you then look for easier things to do? If so, you shouldn't even do it and waste your time." She would laugh and it's obvious that *if we wanted results, we must practice our muscles, and expect pain through the process, that's where the growth comes.*

It was the self-control, determination, and persistence that led me to great results: from being upset and unconfident to being joyful, confident, and powerful. I made it because I knew what I needed. I wanted to gain my confidence and regain my health, physically and mentally. When you know what you need and why you need it, you change and switch what you need to what you want. It helps you to create a healthy desire in you. If you only achieve what you want and do not look at what you need, your life is going to be a mess. Because what you want may not be what you need at all. For example, if a baby asks for a glass of wine when you are drinking it, what will happen if the baby gets what he or she wanted? This is just a little example, but you get what I mean.

What are you facing now that makes you feel so painful? You have choices to make: one is to make excuses you do not need to change, and keep whatever it is, keep complaining; Two, start to try to once it gets too hard, you give up because to give up is easier than making efforts to change, at least you tried. Or three, you choose to be the leader of your life. Since you are a leader in your life, you have the liability to lead the right decisions. I believe you would love to take the third option, which is to lead with self-control and execute it with high determination and persistence. **"I decided to do the right thing, not the easy thing. How about you?"**

Did you ever live in deplorable family conditions and in a terrible physical environment? What decision will you make in that situation? I lived in a very ordinary and financially struggling family. Some of the physical environment was extremely bad.

For example, did you ever see a toilet without a bowl? Did you ever need to go out to find a bathroom when you couldn't hold it in the middle of the night? No streetlights. You had to use a torch. And the toilet wasn't modern; you had to hold your breath every single time you went in, and you also had to be mindful of stepping on the 'Number Twos'...
... It was horrible, right? I would laugh when I talk about this now, but it was so painful. Not joking, I still had nightmares about searching for a clean bathroom to go to, which was caused by the shadow from my childhood experience.

The other painful experience was that there was no private shower place throughout my childhood. We could not afford to build a shower room in our house, so we had to go to the public shower place all the time. I still remember that my parents worked in a chemical factory where the smell was terrible. It was toxic. But my Mum had to go and work there all day. My Dad was the security guard, so he was a bit luckier that he didn't need to live in the pungent smell right near the machines. My mum was the operator, so she got very sick after that, got lots of strange diseases which I believe many of them were resulting from the bad working environment- the toxic smells of those chemicals. There were many days when my sister and I had to go with our parents to the public shower place in the factory, and it was amongst machines, and it was super noisy. No exaggeration. The smell was so bad that every time I felt like I could die there being poisoned. Honestly not sure how we went through all of these when I was still so little. I got choices. One, to complain, feel sorry for me, for my family, or two, to focus on goodness and find a way out. I chose two.

Because of those poor conditions, I spoke to myself every day that I had to learn harder and work harder, to create a better environment for my family and I. I realized that because of the poor conditions, I barely chose to complain and be miserable about what I was going through; neither did I choose to blame my parents or anybody else. Initially, it was frustrating, but as time went by, I turned my eyes to the grateful things. I chose to appreciate and love more. *If it's dark everywhere, a tiny light can light up the room, thus, don't give up trying to make a difference, it's easier than you think.* In the other words, *we do not need much to be happy and grateful*, just a decision is enough. Once my eyesight was too full to see any more negativity or bitterness, my life was only filled with light and joy.

When life gets too harsh, and there seems to be no way you can get out, find a way to enjoy it because, with a joyful heart, all problems will become no problem. I chose to be the extraordinary person who could get through all these difficulties, and I told myself that if I could get through these, nothing else I could not. That was when the real power in me started to show.

What are the things you are suffering but seems never going to change? Will you try to change your mind to live your life with a joyful heart? Tell yourself that good things are coming your way if your situation is so painful, because no situation will last forever. Just hold on, because everything is going to pass, that includes your bad situations.

Thank you for listening to my stories, how about you? *Do you ever feel you are not good enough? Do you ever feel that nobody loves you? Will you do me a favour? Give yourself a big smile completely and boldly in the mirror; embrace and accept yourself; believe that you are just perfectly beautiful!* **Kill the negative thoughts in you that are stopping you from loving yourself and others. Do not let these thoughts trouble you.**

The decision of self-love and loving people brought me many more friends in life. My relationships went to the peak when I make this decision in anywhere and anytime. When people feel you are loved, loving, and lovable, you just attract everyone to be close to you. That was exactly what happened to me.

I am not encouraging us to be people pleasers, but if we make good decisions in life, we get better results in life. Did you hear about the **butterfly effect**? (in chaos theory) the phenomenon whereby a minute localized change in a complex system can have large effects elsewhere. A decision can change your whole life.

When I was suffering, I felt helpless and vulnerable, and I would ask myself: "Why? Why am I always the one?" I always felt that I was always the unlucky one. However, as time went by, I realized that I did not know what happened to others doesn't mean that I could assume that they had a perfect life. It does not mean that they are not suffering. It simply means that I am not alone because everyone suffers, and there is no fixed measure or judge that can weigh whose suffering is more. Because everyone suffers from different things.

Nevertheless, the more I suffered, the more I realized that all these sufferings were the perfect opportunities for me to *decide* whether to 'ruin' or to 'grow' my life. I wish I could use a few words to tell you how my childhood was and what things I experienced to reflect what you are participating in your life. I did not want to share the sad stories but I chose to, because I knew that I needed to. I needed to because you needed to hear about it, and if it's not you, there will be someone who needs to know.

I do not know you in person, but I know how you feel, and I could see your frustration because we are all humans. **No matter how** perfect you think others' life looks, none of them is perfect, and we are all experiencing similar pains, feelings, and thoughts even though we live in different places and have different lifestyles. Don't believe me? Ask anyone in your life if they never suffer anything?

My friend, make a good decision today, say to yourself: **"I decided to be an extraordinary person who can always love and shine. I focused on being a better version of myself and did not compare."**

If I tell you that you are born to be extraordinary, but to choose to be extraordinary does not mean you will get everyone to agree with all your opinions? Nor can you delight everyone; Will you still want to be extraordinary? *Being extraordinary is not competing with anybody else. It is simply to know that you have a choice, and you choose to be extraordinary and bring excellence to everything you do. Be the best version of yourself and accept yourself entirely and boldly despite the noises around you.*

Being extraordinary is not expecting to suffer less but even if suffering more, you are still courageous to get stronger each time. *You are always ready to grow from any pain, not let the pain grow.* If you are not ready to suffer temporary pain or setbacks, you are not prepared to be extraordinary, and you will suffer pain in the long term. When better opportunities come, you are not ready to handle them. Alternatively, on the other hand, if you are ready to be extraordinary, make a good decision now. Keep this unique spirit, be a changemaker, to make a difference in this world. **Be still and firm with your 'Skim Milk' choice in life, do not doubt.**

Whenever you are facing setbacks of 'no choice left', please remember the 'Skim Milk' moment, that *you always have a choice! Your choice is your decision. What you decide is what is going to happen!* Remember that the 'Skim Milk' moment will bring people's judgment. Expect the noise! The 'Skim Milk' moment is an excellent opportunity to decide the next step in your life. Be courageous to order your 'skim milk.' It is the only way to live a complete life and be an authentic YOU. **If you fear being hated by people, it's impossible for you to discover the true YOU either.**

A great leader makes good decisions, not excuses. Are you going to make better decisions in your life? Do you want to unlock your self-empowerment to live a joyful life and be a joyful leader in life? Here is your next decision to make. If your answer is yes, then start by accepting yourself, knowing who you are, and being courageous to be YOU!

Are you ready to choose to love completely? Because to find the joyful leader in you starts with loving completely.

CHAPTER TWO

The beauty in you.

Lead to love and understand.

No puzzle is too complicated for love to solve, and no one is too harsh for love to soften.

We live in one of the most challenging times regarding people's connections. It seems there is more hate than love, more judgment than understanding. Part of the main reason is that people have become busy with their businesses. The world has too many attractions and distractions that drag people away from real life. The computer, the smartphone, Netflix, and online games, are all fantastic inventions to entertain people. Still, the good nature we are supposed to be is to be part of the community and be in real social life. We slowly became more selfish than caring; We gradually lost our outstanding social skills in real life. People find happiness and joy and release their hate to social media instead. The other reason is that we watch too much news because media and newsletters are so common nowadays. That is why we are losing the capability and the skills to love and understand truly.

How to love completely? To a leader like me, I believe one of the most magical and powerful joyful leadership actions is 'love'. The love I am talking about is not 'you love fish' but you eat fish; it is not passion; it's not you love something, you bought it, then you didn't take care of it anymore when passion burns out. None of these is real love. The love I am talking about is much more than that. It is not a noun; it is a verb.

Do you find it's hard to love and appreciate yourself completely? I had the same challenges. When I was very young, I hated how I looked, especially when people started comparing me with those around me. My sister was always the one who was praised for her pretty face. I was the insignificant one because of my overweight issue. Not just my face, but also my outlook, as I did not even have many new clothes to wear. 90% of my clothes were second handed from others or my sister.

As I grew up more, the more I admired other people's beauty, the more I lost sight of myself. I did one of the dumbest things in the world because I wanted to have longer eyelashes. I ended up listening to a rumour which said if you wanted longer, just cut them, and the more you cut, the longer they will regrow out. Once I cut one side of my eyelashes, I immediately regretted it so much and blamed myself: "What are you doing, Silly girl?" Of course, that didn't work, and I ended up carrying unbalanced eyelashes until they grew back. But well, I believe all of us could have done something silly to make ourselves look better or prettier.

I could not stop comparing myself with my sister and all people who seemed to look better. Until one day, I was so update because of doubting my own look and felt worthless. I was standing in front of the mirror, looking at myself, for a long time, thinking, how will I love this person there? There were two choices I could have made. One, I would just give up and say: You know what, I wasn't beautiful enough because I wasn't born into a great family, or any other excuses and complaints I could make and think of. Two, I could start to learn and practice how to accept myself and love myself more.

Thankfully, *I did go with the second choice*. I started to appreciate little things about myself. I began to adore myself with self-encouragement. When I didn't see myself as pretty, I started to find where I think they were pretty. The more I tried, the more I could find out. It took some time, but after practice, bit by bit, time after time, I started to appreciate every single part of my body. The magical part is, when I started to accept myself more and felt more confident, the confidence made me more beautiful than ever.

My self-talk language becomes like: "You know what, you have such beautiful eyes, lips, and everything; they may not be what others think as perfect separately, but when combined, they are unique, making a perfect you!! Nobody would have got your look, but one day when they find out your inner beauty, everybody will love to appreciate your beauty." That self-talk was so powerful that I even remembered one day, I said to myself in the mirror: "You are just so beautiful inside and out." That's what I believe about myself, leading me closer every day to becoming what I believe.

I didn't mention this to anyone: the look of my teeth bothered me for a long-time. It took me years to accept that my weird-looking teeth are part of me. I even got compliments from people saying they loved my teeth. Little did I remember I had struggled for at least eight years, smiling without opening my mouth, particularly while taking photos. Now, I can always open my mouth almost in every photo. No hesitation, completely and boldly. ***My teeth didn't change, but my attitude did.***

I found a secret that only to love others can I love myself completely! Without love, you cannot achieve any successful leadership. It is impossible to switch on our inner power without loving ourselves. It's hard to love if we don't know who we are. Why are we so emotional and vulnerable but strong and courageous sometimes? Why can't we live a life full of joy and peace, but we must still keep feeling distracted, insecure, stressed, angry, or sad? There are different answers to these questions. But 'love' can definitely be the solution to all of these issues.

So, the way that can solve all these problems starts with finding your purpose. And the purpose is bigger than yourself, and that is to lead by loving people.

I started to own powerful feelings and self-love, I started to own the power to love and give too. I realized after the self-talk that my inner beauty makes me confident in my outlook and inside beauty. **That's the day I decided to switch focus from working on my outer beauty to working on my inner beauty, which is the inside of my soul, knowing how to love people.** Because only when you decide to love someone would you have the capability to love yourself, because if you want someone love you, you should always love them first.

I shifted my whole perspective from focusing on myself to others, which made me feel so powerful in love. Don't get me wrong, I still think that only if you have the power to love yourself, then can you be capable of loving others, but somehow, they exist at the same time. The power of self-love and loving others help each side. In short, if you want to be loved, love someone, and then you will get to learn the superpower on how to love yourself too. **Self-love is powerful, but selfless love is powerfully magical.**

How could I work in the same industry for 20 years but still love it? If my purpose is only going for achieving more things for myself, I would easily have given up and felt worthless. I would easily get bored with what I do. As a human being, our flesh is easily distracted, and our mind is easily going to the negative side if we don't have something in us to guide and hold us to the right direction. We can make so many bad decisions if we only think for ourselves instead of each other.

Instead, every time when I felt needed by others and when I did something for others, I felt happy and valuable. If I think for others before I simply do something for myself, the outcome will always turn out to be win-win. It helps me to make so many wise decisions. As a leader for so many years, if I need to conclude one word to be a good leader,

I would say it is love. It is the love I have for all people around me. The love to my boss and my team members. There is a famous saying: One for all, all for one. That is the key to leading a better life. Because of love, no matter what happens, things will end up well.

Joyce Meyer's quote: "Being selfish and happy cannot exist at the same time." It's very true. My life experience tells me that only love can kick the ass of your selfishness and discover your unselfishness. You can then be truly happy. This is applying to my own life with my family too. Every time when I forget about the 'love language' to my family, I forget about how to love myself too. When I treat my hubby or children impatiently, I am also impatient with myself. It can be a day in heaven or hell, depending on how I choose to respond that day. If I choose to lead to love and understand my family that day, it will be a day in heaven. Or on the opposite, it would end up being a day of disaster.

I am not talking about being super unrealistic to love anyone at any time (yes if we can.), however, it is more about an attitude and an action for you to take and that final ultimate beneficiary will be YOU. The questions here are: "Do you love yourself enough? Who are you, and why do you need to love others when you think you should love yourself more? What type of people do you love? How do you love yourself and others?"

Ahead of love, you must *know* and *understand* that person first, right? Without knowing or understanding, it's impossible to just love. I am going to share with you what I found in my life, and I believe they could help you answer most of the confusion you are facing when you have to deal with billions of people on earth. When I discovered these and changed my perspective of seeing things, my life became much more joyful, loved, grateful, and complete! Yes, complete. If it is not full, 99% or 99.9%, there will be a 1% or 0.1% chance that you cannot enjoy your life 100%. Don't let that tiny chance creep in.

<u>The first thing</u> I discovered is that **I choose to love because**

we are all different. I choose to be the one who loves people and learns from everyone's differences!

Are we different? Yes, we are! We are all beautifully different!

It's so amazing that there are about 7.75 billion people on earth, but none of us is the same! Even though someone can do plastic surgery to get similar looks as their favourite stars. There's still nobody on the planet who will be the same. Our faces and bodies change every day because of our physical movement, and the things we eat and do. It makes it harder for anyone who wants to copy the same face and body from someone. We can say: They look so much alike or similar, but we cannot say they are exactly the same, because we are all unique.

As some of you are aware of my business, one of the motivational reasons behind it is that I have a huge passion for people and multinational business. My dream is always to bring people together from everywhere in the world so that we live together and show love and respect to each other all the time; no selfishness, only peace, and harmony. I am so eager to see that in my network business, we have every different individual from the world who looks different, with diverse backgrounds and cultures sitting in the same room and being in the same global family.

With my past international traveling experiences, I enjoyed attending all the global conferences to meet people from everywhere. I found every one of them is so beautiful in different ways. That's when I realized that I have a great gift of seeing the best part of each person. **Believe me, through thousands of people I met in life, I am confident to say that everyone has something in them that you can fall in love with!** If you believe it, try to use a different perspective to see people and know people from now on.

To me, one of the best things about work that didn't make me feel I was working but more like enjoying life is that I can meet someone.

Whoever that is, I can listen to their stories and share my stories. We can build up connections and friendships, grow and learn from each other. Whenever that opportunity of connecting to anybody came up, I would love to take it and make time for that person. Each person is valuable and each of them deserves respect and time from me. That was one of the best decisions I ever made. I led my life to always remain teachable and growable from anyone at any time. This is also very important to my leadership journey. Joyful leadership starts with seeing the beauty in people.

You will ask, how am I going to see beauty in people and in myself? Everyone has a different background, education, and experience and could have different standards and choices. But I have some important messages for you today! **Whether young or old, short or tall, white or black, straight or gay, rich or poor, disabled or abled, uneducated or well-educated. You are one of us, human beings.** We all have doubts as humans, right? Are you doubting your inner or outside beauty and struggling with self-confidence? Are you feeling that you have nothing different but just ordinary human beings?

First, you must have heard true stories that a handsome man married an ordinary-looking woman, or a beauty married someone whom many people think he's ugly? There is an interesting article you can read: https://justrichest.com/14-beautiful-celebrities-who-married-ugly-spouses/, posted by Amiral Daniel.

It talked about 14 beautiful celebrities who married ugly spouses. I do not agree that the spouses are that truly ugly because everyone's standard is different. I believe there are inner beauties that we cannot see but their spouse could see. You see, there are so many different opinions in the society where we live. In fact, many who don't have very outstanding looking do have very beautiful hearts.

We can have both, but I always believe that **A true beauty sees beauty in others too**! If we judge people as ugly, that is also reflecting the ugly side of our own. It doesn't mean we cannot speak of the true feeling;

it is simply saying that if we want to be beautiful inside out, we should start with small things like appreciating and seeing beauty in others.

You'd be interested to know how our brain responds to beauty. Check out the article: How the Brain Responds to Beauty – Scientific American By Jason Castro on February 2, 2021 here: https://www.scientificamerican.com/article/how-the-brain-responds-to-beauty/

Do you know why our self-doubts always come so often? Because we all subconsciously believe that public aesthetics is the right standard. Everyone is pursuing to be perfect. So was I. Sometimes I am still pursuing perfection. But please do not ever believe that in our real life, there is one person who has a perfect life with no ups and downs. It only exists in Disneyland, which is why we call it a wonderland. Do not ever believe that everybody makes the right decisions all the time just like all the perfect protagonists in the movie. Everybody makes mistakes and wrong decisions. But all of these don't change the fact that you are perfectly different. It is so fascinating to see almost 8 billion people on earth. Everyone is different looking, even though the twins could have some differences. Isn't that precious and beautiful?

Your beauty of being different:

- You are beautiful because you are different in many ways: background, culture, and experience.
- You are beautiful because nobody can take your identity away, even though sometimes you might feel judged.
- You are beautiful because nobody can play the best role of YOU except for yourself. People can replace your job, and your title, but they can never replace YOU as yourself!!
- You are beautiful because you have your own stories that others don't; that built up the special YOU!!
- You are beautiful, simply because you are unique and just **perfect as who you are.**

The Joyful Leader In You

Do you have any of these moments? "Oh, I wish I could have her eyes, skin colour, and hair!" "I wish I have his life!" "I wish I could be him!" "I wish... ...!" So many of us have icons to chase and people to look up to, but there is always a mess behind the perfect version of everyone that you can't see. You and me too. We all have messes, no matter how successful we may look outwardly.

I was ever longing to become someone else too when I was little. Whenever I watched a TV show, I would choose one of the main characters to worship and start trying to act like that person on TV. I enjoyed imagining being the hero that I dreamed of being. Many kids are fans of Elsa from Frozen and fans of Disney princesses nowadays. Avengers' movies by Marvel Studios and so on. Adults too! There are countless fans of these fantastic TV/Movie heroes.

But there's now a famous saying: Never meet your heroes. Why? Because the icons you like are just fictional characters and perfect versions to feed the audience. The rare we can find in real life, the more precious it becomes, and the more demand that means, which is why more people want to watch and chase things that rarely exist in real life. I didn't worship icons anymore when I became a teenager, and I spent more time learning from each character's shining point instead. For example, what were the good attitude that the character had? What were the wise decisions they made?

There's one interesting fact that I discovered during my work experience meeting multinational people of all ages and backgrounds. People in Asia particularly China (as I was born in China) almost everyone there wants pale skin colour. But on the other side of the planet, like in the USA/Australia, people love tan skin colour. They do fake tan! In China, we call it dark! But in most cities and countries in Asia, some people even take vitamin C treatment to make them look whiter! Snow write is their goal and dream! Then funny enough, I appreciate and love the tan colour too. I love all different types of colours because they represent their beauty differently. People from everywhere in the world have a special and unique beauty in them.

Don't you realize that things will only become precious and more expensive when they are less or rare? Like a diamond? Yes, I am talking to you. The difference you have is a diamond! You are even more precious than a diamond.

The other amusing fact is that foreigners are famous in China and highly welcomed by most of the majority. You see, so many European or African looks were popular, and easier to find ways of living because they are a small number of people and special when they go to a different country. It is the same if you are from Asia and everyone around you is born in the same place with the same blood source. It makes you less unique, right? But when you appear in a group of other nationalities, you shine with your difference. I loved the moment I attended international conferences when I was always the ONLY. I was always the only female leader and one of the youngest among all the other leaders.

Another interesting fact is that if you check some internationally famous faces, such as the famous Hollywood actress Gong Li from eastern countries, they are indeed considered unnoticed in most eastern people's eyes. Some Chinese models are even criticized as ugly to the eastern aesthetic, but people from western countries love them and think they are beautiful. You see how different the outcome can be when we have different perspectives and standards.

Hair Colours! I saw so many stories that Asian love to have blonde hair, but I also saw those who initially had lighter colours want something darker! Don't get me wrong, there's nothing wrong with dyeing your hair, and I am doing it too. I am one of those who want to enjoy different outlooks! I love to change my outfit or make-up look daily to feel fresh. That is fine because you follow your heart and know what you want. The point I want to make here is: **different colours of skin or hair are so beautiful in different ways!! Various looks and** cultures are so beautiful and charming in their own ways! They are the best gifts we could ever have. Small things like this are essential!

Do you know what people want the most!? Why are they always dissatisfied? Or appreciate what they have? *You see, people only wish for things they don't have yet. But when we keep chasing something we don't have and focusing on it, we tend to forget how many beautiful things we already have quickly.*

Asian prefer pale skin!

European or American prefer tan colours!

People live in the countryside, longing for city life.

People live in the city, longing for the countryside life!

People who lost a job want a job.

People who have jobs want to quit their job.

Single people wish to marry.

Married people wish to have a single life.

Some people have kids, but they admire those who don't have kids;

Some people desperately want kids but struggle to get pregnant, and some have to try IVF.

There are things on and on.

We are different, and we must choose to embrace our difference! The more I accepted everyone with diverse backgrounds and cultures around me, the more I found charm and fun in life. Life is no longer boring, and I am in love with people who have things I don't and who experienced things that I never had. **Because when I embrace and appreciate others' differences, it helps me to embrace all the things I have and not feel lacking for the things I don't. Our life is always like a mirror, and it is always a reflection.**

To activate your leadership capability, you must change your perspective to see things and people differently. Embrace all the differences and enjoy the experiences. Don't try to get everyone to be like you;

enjoy and embrace the differences. One of the passions behind my international business was that there's a power to bring a group of different cultures and backgrounds together. There's power in unity!

The second thing I found is: *I choose to love because we are all the same!*

Are we the same? Yes, we are because we are all humans! We are not pigs, trees, toys, or plants. We are humans!

I found it fascinating that most body parts are combined in pairs. Two eyes to see, one brain (left and right brains), one nose (2 nose holes) to breathe, two ears to listen, and one mouth (2 lips) to talk. The point here is that we are the same types. It is like pigs are pigs, cats are cats, mushrooms are mushrooms, and vegetables are vegetables. **We are not plants or animals but humans.** I always make fun of and ask my daughter, what do you think the alien will look at us? Ugly or beautiful? Cute or funny? Do you think they will see us as aliens? Yes, they will. They will be scared by our looks. Imagine you see someone with their butt on their head and they talk with their butt or if they have four arms and three legs!! It takes you time to accept, right?

We are all humans, no matter if we were born from a good or better family or place, we are hot-blooded people, and we have our common human languages: Body language, Music, Singing, Dancing, smiling, crying, laughing, screaming, shouting, weeping. And so much more!

We are also brothers and sisters on earth, the planet we live on. You have the right to choose whom you want to be close with and to live with, but you cannot deny that we are all the same – human beings!

We all have feelings! We are all born from our parents, whether you have ever met them! We all have gifts, desires, and dreams!

The judgment we make about one person is never fair! It was the same when you were or felt judged by someone, as we can never see through the other's whole life! Everyone has a different story to tell. Every coin has two sides.

The biggest thing that helps me not judge or feel better when people judge me is **sympathy.** It is an essential ability for a joyful leader to show Compassion. By realizing that we can feel how each other feels. We feel sad when others feel sad, as we know we can have the same feeling, we had that feeling before, or we could have experienced the same feeling someday, so we want to do something to make them feel better. Compassion comes from love. Love produces sympathy and forgiveness that can bring peace to our hearts, minds, and souls.

I am always passionate about things and everything I do! Sometimes I didn't dig too much about why, but I always found a way to enjoy it so that I could love what I do or do what I love!

It took me a while to realize that my passion wasn't after anything else but people! The relationship with people! It's the value I could bring to people, and the opportunity to know more people, help more people, or learn from them brings me all passion and joy!

Sympathy is also one of the reflections of the love you have for people. It is one of the vital successful elements to be a great leader. In short, to become a great leader in your life and work, you must learn to love and show sympathy.

I always believe there are no bad people, only some good people who may make bad choices or decisions! If you understand what I am saying. Trust me, we are all different but the same in other ways!

Did you ever prank or do something to someone, and you felt terrible afterward? I had to confess that no matter how behaved I was in my childhood and how good I am now, I did naughty things too.

Did you ever do something terrible like stealing? Put your hands up if you never do something wrong. No hands will go up because we all made bad choices. I ever stole one of my auntie's money which was the worst experience ever. I barely got money from my parents to buy snacks, but all others had. I couldn't stop getting the money when I saw them in the drawer; even though it was just a few dollars, I felt so ashamed and unhappy afterward. I was fearful and worried that someone would find out, so they did.

I confessed my guilt and cried for a very long time, feeling like I was the worst person in the world. After then, I became quiet for a long time, ad I started to learn to understand why being honest is so important. That has become one of my core values in my life from then on. That was once and NEVER. I was only 5 or 6. Do I call myself the wrong person? No. Our bad choices and mistakes don't define us. On the other side, that experience helped me to become an honest person ever.

Did you ever get cheated on or betrayed by anyone? Put your hands up if you have never had the experience. All adults should have had that experience or felt that before. I got people who stole my wallet and my phone. I got people who said they would borrow money from me and give it back, but they didn't. I got people and friends who promised things but never did. These could all break my trust and belief in people, but why didn't I? Because I always believe that there were so many more unknown stories behind what a person you thought was 'bad' could have been going through.

People will never stop judging based on things you did or mistakes you made BEFORE! But it doesn't change the FACT that you never stop moving on and learning to be a better you NOW!

My youngest uncle – my mum's youngest brother has one broken leg, his wife left him, his son suffered mental illness, and this whole family is so broken. But I still show very high respect to him and love him because, in my eyes, I could see so much of his strengths, talents, and independence! He started to be self-taught to be a mechanic. He could fix devices or auto parts with self-taught skills when he was only 20. He could fix all the motorbikes or bikes, even any machines. He even made some of his machines and designed his own bikes. He was so good-looking, but he never cared about his look; instead, he cared about the people around him. He was one of the most loyal and kindest people I ever saw. Unfortunately, his marriage didn't work out, and his wife left him all the responsibilities to take alone. He is so independent, and he still never complains. He is just one of the kindest people I could ever see. Should we judge him? Judge him a failure because of his family situation? Or should we appreciate him for his efforts and kind heart?

I love people's stories because everyone has at least one that could touch me, and they have at least one thing I could learn from. So, I started learning and growing secretly but joyfully.

Highly recommended you to read this article from Melanie Greenberg Ph.D. **from** The Mindful Self-Express. **The title:** 10 Research-Based Truths About People in Love

https://www.psychologytoday.com/us/blog/the-mindful-self-express/201311/10-research-based-truths-about-people-in-love

1. We all need to be loved and to be in love. In Melanie's article, it mentioned 10 facts based on research: Love is different from passion or lust.
2. Love is both a momentary feeling and a long-term state of mind.
3. Building lasting relationships take work.
4. We can increase our capacity to love.
5. It's not just in your head.
6. If we focus on love, we can enhance it.
7. It is not a fixed quantity.
8. It is not unconditional.
9. It is contagious.
10. Love is not necessarily forever, but it can be.

For point 8, it said that one of the preconditions for loving feelings is a sense of safety and trust. **Love does not have to be a spouse's love; it can be love in various kinds of relationships.**

To be a leader, you MUST learn how to LOVE others. **To love others is to love ourselves!** Keep believing and loving people because it will make you different from others and ultimately make you the great leader of your life. Because you cannot offer yourself the love that you need from others, it is different. We all need relationships, and we all need each other. Every relationship needs mutual ways. You can only be a successful leader if you know how to love others. To lead yourself well starts with loving yourself. Loving yourself is to love someone as well. Because purely selfish love for ourselves cannot make us feel loved or happy, we all need someone to love and love us.

My marriage with my husband has been more than 13 years, we also had some arguments and fights, but it was minimal. No seven years' itchiness, we have been thrilled together. The key to our happy marriage is 'love.' No matter what happens, if we show love to each other, any other issues will become no issue. Because we both will try to communicate and let each other feel more loved.

Whenever I choose to be self-centred, I would lose sight of how to love others and myself. Instead, when I started to take care of others and put others first, I immediately felt more loved and could find a better way to love people again. It is like a win-win game- an organic love circle. If you start one thing, the other will be benefited. 'In lifting others, we rise' is my business network slogan. It helps to create so much love in our network community.

My passion will never go away because of my love for people! Trust me, if you start to love people, real love, selfless love, your life will only be better! You shall find a significant shift in yourself! You are no longer self-centred! You will find all your love for people come to you and make you more complete! Cherish everyone in your life! Don't judge them by their mistakes but learn things from each of them! Because everyone has a unique story that can inspire you, and be hungry to hear some of your testimonials to encourage them!

Yes, loving others and yourself is the answer. However, it is always easier to say than to do, right? Let alone changing the situation or people; we also can be hurt by people all the time; People can always say or do things that destroy your joy. But do you know you always have a choice not to be offendable and to choose joy? Because being a leader is a joyful role, so you must **find joy** in your leadership life to enjoy this journey. *Seek, and you will find.*

CHAPTER THREE

Joyful Leadership Myth.

Lead not to be offended.

The biggest enemy of joy is to be offended. When we are offended, we believe what people say about us is accurate. Practicing our anti-anger muscles starts by knowing our strengths and weaknesses. **People who lack nothing will not be offended because they already know their strengths and weakness well.** If we are offended, our self-empowerment will get stuck. Our full potential talents will only be able to manifest when we feel complete.

Many people have been chasing happiness their whole life, but they lose it soon. Happiness is a short-term satisfaction that is easy to expire and can be on and off quickly. It restricts the situations and conditions. Happiness can't be shared because it is minimal and conditional. If you have a happy life, you can't share the happiness with others because they are not getting everything you get unless you share some of your material things, unless it is under some conditions. In other words, it is conditional. A person can be happy because he buys a nice gift for himself, but he may not have joy in him. A kid can be so happy when he gets his favourite ice-cream. See, all happy people are experiencing smooth, easy, and conditional environments. In other words, when the environment or condition changes, they are no longer satisfied. Happiness doesn't last very long.

But Joy is different. It has longer validity, is unconditional, it is unconquerable if you are determined to keep it. It doesn't restrict you from any good or bad circumstances. For example, you can find a person who lives in a super lousy environment with limited food and entertainment, but he can be full of joy. Joy can be shared and doubled. Share the pain, and your pain gets less. Share joy, and your joy increases more. You don't have to share any material things. You share it and spread it by changing your attitude and response! Like when someone shares his joyful story with his friends, the joy will be increased and extended to all.

Like everyone, I had always been chasing long-lasting happiness. I worked hard, improved my condition, and my life was quite happy, but whenever I had a bad day, or someone at work was rude to me, it seemed my life wasn't that happy anymore. Then I found out that our enemy of pain isn't happiness but joy. Happiness doesn't take our pain away. Joy is a pain relief that brings us happiness and peace simultaneously. One of the best symbols of joy is gratitude. When you are grateful, there will be irreplaceable inner joy.

How to choose joy? Does it mean avoiding people you don't like or doing things you don't like, then you will have joy? Do you want to change your circumstance or focus on changing your inner perspective and response?

It is more common that people love to circle each other in different groups and select their group to be with. I was in that place too. It is good to be surrounded by great people, and it helps us to become better, but we also need to be aware that if our life is full of people talking only good things about us and always agree with us, our life no longer has much space to improve or grow. Our eyes will be blindfolded. We can no longer see things from two sides. We are comfortable if we choose to hang out with a small group of people. But our world will be too small to fit bigger things and purposes because we will subconsciously set our limits in the comfortable zone. Get uncomfortable!

The other possible but hurtable truth is you can miss great opportunities if you only choose to meet some specific and similar group of people, live in your safe friendship zone, and never have any breakthrough. One of the favourite things I'd love to do is to hang out with various backgrounds of people and global cultures. I got friends from 20 years + younger than me to 40 years + older than me. Sometimes, some of them said something straightforward to me that might hurt my feeling, and if I had chosen to be offended, they'd also stop being honest with me, and I could also decide to shut the door and kick them out of my world. Luckily, I didn't. You would be surprised that most of these people became my besties and ended up being the most extended and valuable friends in my life. You never know how big the impact that one person in your life could make in your life! The key is rather than avoiding them and hiding from people you may not like, the best is to practice our **not offended muscles.**

Besides, we don't always get to choose which people we want to live nearby or will meet in our life. So rather than ticking out everyone and finding their imperfection, why not choose to understand and accept the fact that we don't need to delight or be delighted by everyone? When we are no longer offended easily, we become more humble, learnable, and growable. We will lead a life with unbreakable joy.

How do we practice our *not offended* muscles? How do we know ourselves completely so that we can naturally respond joyfully? After all, if we can never be offended, our relationship management will hit a higher level.

First, as a leader in life and career, to not get offended easily, here are some practical tips for maintaining a good

relationship that I found super helpful. I have been using these methods in my life (for all kinds of relationships: Friends, Colleagues, Parents and kids, Partners, Husband and wife, Leaders and team.) It is called **LSC.**

    2 Ls (Love & Listening for Listening)
    2 Ss (Show Compassion & Spend Qualified Time)
    3 Cs (Care, Change Not & Connecting before correcting)

Love

The most powerful word is LOVE. We mentioned **leading to love** in the previous chapter. Here I'd like to explore its magic for you to be a joyful leader in both life and career.

    Someone says love can bring all good things.
    Someone says love can solve all problems.
    Someone says love can conquer all difficulties.
    Someone says that God is 'Love' because he loves us.
    What are your understandings of love?

To me, except for what the above concludes, love is magical, but love is a 'verb' more than a 'noun.' To love is easy to say but hard to act sometimes, which is why we all must build up our love languages and find people's love languages because everybody could have different demands on how to be loved. That is also why we need to practice. If love is so easy, we don't need to practice, and all relationships should work perfectly, but we all know that's not the case.

By the way, the misguide from Disney Princess movies was a big problem to guide all new generations, including myself, that it always says that love at first sight and living happily ever after. They could get married the second day they met, which is beautiful but ridiculous. I love Disney movies so much, but if you are reading my book and haven't found your Mr. or Ms. Right, don't expect that you could marry someone with whom you fell in love at first sight, ok? What if that person already got married? What if they want to have a playful relationship? Love takes time, and finding someone you can rely on for your whole life also takes time.

To love all people from the deep of your heart; To love where you work from the bottom of your heart; To love what you do; If you can, choose what you love; if you can't, love what you do. Either way will bring you happiness and joy.

I am not referring to the spouse's love; to love all people is a more generous love. I mean the ability to love people unconditionally, not your love for your partner but the love you can have for everyone in your life.

One of the best ways to learn how to love is to embrace people's love, train our ability to love, then enjoy the process of love. It can sometimes cause pain, but we shall always grow from it. After all, there was a time that we ever loved and were loved. After each failed relationship, you will mature more than at any other time when you are waiting to become mature. The bad news is that to love someone will potentially cause hurt, but the good news is that only being fearless to love can make you understand what love truly means.

Love is always the base and core of all relationships. It is the greatest and most workable thing I used in my life and career, such as my ability to be a great salesperson and my soft leadership skills. However, rather than 'love language,' I would use more 'love action.' Things like the below can genuinely help to experience more love and helps with any relationships.

- To give without expecting returns.
- To not over-promise.
- To spend time together.
- To respect each other's decisions and choices.
- To control ourselves instead of trying to control others by using 'love' as an excuse.

- To forgive each other quickly and move on, allow time to heal.
- To be willing to listen.
- To be true but be kind.
- To encourage
- To support
- To understand
- To not envy
- To celebrate others' goodness and success

The list can be very long, and it's impossible for us to do everything all the time and to be perfect, but we can conclude one thing, which is **to love others as we want to be loved**. If you understand this word, you will make wise and helpful decisions for everything you do in all relationships.

It's the same for your career too. **For employers, treat your staff the way you want to be treated.** The world's best leaders never take their employees for granted. A business can last for longer, not just because of the great leader but also because the great leader loves their staff and treat them well. You must admit that business owners have no company or CEO without their team. Even yourself is one of the staff in the company. The easiest way to figure out how to treat them is to ask yourself if you do something to your staff, what if it happens to you? Is that good or bad? You shall then find answers straight away.

For employees, treat your company and other people the way you want to be treated. If you are an employee, always think for the company how to bring more business and money. Only if your company and your boss earn more can you get more. Trust me, as long as they see your value, the wise business owners will reward you; If they don't, that boss doesn't deserve you to work together.

Give time to both your employer and yourself. Be patient, and while you are exploring and contributing, you need to cherish the free resources to use and practice your leadership skills as if it's your own company. Isn't that lovely if you keep growing and being the leader? This mindset helps you to build up your value and train your leadership skills for your future. It's the best time for you to practice and to get ready, and once the opportunity comes, it will only work if you have already been training or you would have to wait longer. Many new starters were too rushed to be the boss or too scared to take more lead of their minds.

I always do my job as if it is my own company, all the time. I started as an operation staff to handle shipments between Shenzhen and Taiwan. The boss gave me 100% freedom, authority, and trust to run, and I took significant ownership and leadership. I treated everything well and thoughtfully because I always believed in 'no pain, no gain.; if I am gold, I can shine anywhere I go; If I am not shining yet, absorb light each day, and one day, I will shine.

In six months, I was promoted to customer service manager simply because, except for what I needed to do, I supported them whenever I saw opportunities to help others. In a business situation, one colleague made a small mistake that could cause an enormous penalty and the possibility of losing that customer. When I got involved and used a different communication method, we won the customer back and received compliments.

I was then promoted to a business development manager to travel with business owners overseas and to all the conferences. Almost all meetings I had would bring an immediate result, and all overseas partners found my passion and energy. They all feel like it's my own company that I am running. No doubt, in a short time, the company gave me the authority to hire 25 people for my Dep. in a few years. The company owners treated me better as well. When they saw my value and passion for the company and the people around me, they loved me back by giving me more authority and a pay rise. Thus, to me, with a leadership attitude of loving what I do and loving people around me wherever I go. Leadership skill – the ability to love makes my career exceptionally well-developed.

In short, if you can understand love and use any of the 'love actions' in your life, it will bring magic to your relationships. Start to 'act love' today. You will meet the most charming version of yourself, and what's more, it will build up an organic love circle in your life because life is like a mirror – when you smile at it, it smiles back at you!

Listening for listening – One of the most popular topics nowadays is 'learning how to listen. It should be known how to listen for listening. Even for me, I still have this issue sometimes, even though it's much improved since I had the awareness. The problem was when people hadn't finished speaking, and I couldn't wait to think about what comments I should prepare to comfort, guide, or help them. I do listen for responses, and I do listen for talking as if they need my wisdom and helpful words to make them feel better.

But I am sometimes wrong. I realized that a good relationship needs a listener to be there listening without preparing a response or trying to fix the person talking. Because first, when they share things with you, it doesn't mean they don't understand what is happening. Sometimes it is just that moment they want you to hear their voice and feel them. Second, you will keep one person the same with just one conversation. After listening for listening, the best part is when they ask you to share more, and you can then share helpful tools to help them. That outcome is way more effective than responding to it too quickly. It took me so long to become a better listener, and I am still learning to listen better.

In my corporate career, there are times when a manager sits around the conference room table. When the staff starts to share their thoughts and opinions, the manager jumps in and interrupts by adding his thoughts, trying to give answers, and so on. This type of manager can hardly succeed inspiring or lifting their staff if there are fewer and fewer voices to be raised. Moreover, more and more team members will become quiet and less motivated to get involved because they know their opinions will be judged or ignored.

Show Compassion!
Refrain from judging so quickly! Do you realize we conclude things fast, no matter good or bad? We always assume too soon, no matter what we see or hear. When we see somebody doing something wrong or bad, the first feeling is, "They are bad." Then we shall feel either angry or upset because of that.

As a manager and leader for years, I also faced many challenges in the workplace. If someone delayed their work, made a huge mistake, or was late for work or meetings, I could either be mad at them, let them feel guilty, or choose to show compassion. I remember I was angry at the beginning when that day one team member came late for work without informing me in advance. I was about to blame her in a bossy way, but I chose a different approach this time. Just a quick thought: what if something terrible happens to them? I decided to ask her if she was ok and if there was anything I could help with. She closed the office door. Then she shared all her emotions with me. She just broke up with her boyfriend. I let her release her emotion and comforted her. I also suggest she focus on something that can distract her from the pain. She chose to move on and keep busy, and her performance headed to a better level later. That day I became a better leader and mentor to someone who desperately needed a listener and a guide to move on. She trusted me and respected me more from then on.

There were many other situations in my team, no matter where I worked and leading to show compassion and not judge them so quickly brought me great success in my leadership career. They would share with me what was happening, and sometimes you would be shocked to hear what happened in their life. I had cases where they lost their parents, broke up with their fiancé, struggled with a health issue, had mental health issues, and so on. When I chose sympathy, it brought me so many good people because it helped me forgive quickly and accept that nobody doesn't make mistakes. Nobody is perfect, but showing sympathy drives us closer.

The same methodology applies to the relationships between my family and me. If I don't show sympathy to my partner for what he does wrong, I don't think I could be forgiven by him so quickly when I make a big mistake; If I don't show sympathy to my daughters for what they did wrong, I don't think they would be willing to keep learning and trying. It is unfair to measure anyone by using one thing they do wrong and ignoring many things they do right.

Spending Quality Time, especially bonding one-on-one time, is so important. I am a person who has worked in a cooperative world for a very long. One of the best things I learned from my experience is team building in the workplace. It has various ways to do it. You can organize a lunch or dinner, coordinate a game, or have a one-on-one meeting. When people ask me how I managed to lead my team, family, friends, and community, I realize that spending qualified time (one-on-one) is one of the greatest keys.

Two examples:
First, in the workplace, the team I managed had many conflicts and fights, and they started to hate each other and pointed fingers at each other at their back. I realized I needed to do something, so I arranged an online meeting by playing games. One of the things I did was to ask each of them to list at least one thing they admire about the other person on the team. We all know that everyone has a weakness but also lots of strengths. So rather than encourage them to look at what they don't have, it was powerful to let each other see their good side and appreciate each other. When I saw one team member who used to say terrible things about the other member who started to speak marvellous things

from the bottom of his heart, the other guy was so grateful. They found each other's better version during our team call in a few short minutes. The most unbelievable part is that with the quality time they spent, they started to understand and like more about each other more. After the online game, I even heard that they began to talk to each other directly with honest and appreciative conversations behind the scenes. I was so thrilled with the more vital team spirit!

Many things happen because of a lack of connection, which causes distrust and doubt, which is why the fighting occurs quickly. Instead, for those who know each other deeply, even a silly joke that sounds very bad to the third party does not stir the listener simply because they already have a good connection. Do you worry too much when you make a big joke with your best friend? You won't because you already got a deep connection!

The other example:
In my life as well, I am always a full-time job mum, and since I am always a goal-driven person, I needed to remember to spend enough time with my husband and kids. When we are frustrated with each other easily, that's the Danger Sign that reminds me we should spend more quality time together. It is one of the hardest things to have that awareness and put into the to-do list because you always think that you see each other every day; what's the point of intentionally Spending Time Together while you are already together? Trust me, seeing each other doesn't mean you have a qualified time together. So, once we take that initiative, we will see our relationship heating up again.

If my daughters start to say no very often and show little obedience, that means I need to spend more quality time with them. Because whenever I did, they just became angels. Kids need us to spend time with them to feel truly loved, which is cruel (to the parents' reality, particularly busy parents like me), but magical (to let our children feel more loved, listen to us more, and bring more peace to the family).

Want to own a moment like you found a Genie Lamp that your wishes all come true for the relationships with your family? Spend quality time!

Care –
A healthy relationship starts with love, but we need to care to reflect love. If you love someone, you will care for them intentionally. Unfortunately, there are too many commercial things living in our life nowadays, especially for organizations in the workplace. Many bosses or managers pretend to care for their staff just because they want to keep their jobs well.

When you pretend to care about someone, the outcome can tell, as it turns out much better when you choose to do it intentionally with a true heart. If I could suggest to any organization to have a better team connection or build a stronger team, it must start with leading the team members to love each other and care for each other proactively.

So many people and managers over-commit but under-deliver nowadays because they don't understand proper leadership, how and why they need to care. The right way should be the opposite: Under-commit but over-deliver. Many want a title but don't have a genuine heart to lead and serve their team. Then they pretended to care and do things facially, which could never reach the root of the team spirit. With a true seed, there will grow actual fruits. When people genuinely care about someone, they start with initiatives and action plans. It will show what they are trying to achieve, enough though it is only a small achievement every time. Caring needs a caring heart aligned with loving behaviour, like being willing to offer help and support whenever needed.

The best thing we need to do is not to force ourselves to care for no reason but to find out why. For example, if we don't care for our children, one day, they will be cared by strangers, and most likely, more tragedy could happen to them because they lack care. If we don't care about our staff, they will be cared for by the other company. All investments and values you build on them will be generously transferred to your competitors. If we don't care about our working partners or clients, they will find someone else who cares more for them.

A great relationship needs a genuinely caring heart.
Change Not– 'Change not' means: don't try to change others. Instead of trying to change others, change your attitude and perspective. You would be so surprised at how many relationships are ruined by 'trying to change others, and I was one of them, and I am still in some situations subconsciously. I tried to change the close people around me, especially my kids. I would tell them what to do and how to do it, then expect them to change, and if they didn't, I would end up frustrated. It never works well if I intend to change them. It only works when I change the tune and my attitude, anyhow.

How many of you have the same struggles as this? I once talked to my husband about his morning routines. I thought he should have changed for the better, and how I said it was pushy, and I intentionally tried to force him to say yes to doing what I thought it's right. He said straightforwardly: "Don't try to change me, and I won't try to change you. If you expect me to change, you will always feel disappointed because I don't expect you to be me, either. What if I won't change? Will you still love me?" He is right. I won't give up loving him because he doesn't do what I say, right? Rather than forcing, the better way is influencing.

Thus, instead of trying to change him, I started my daily exercise routine and sent him a link for reference. I said: "Hey, this is what I found, and I think it should be good for you if you want to try. It's up to you, and I will do it, anyway." So, the magic happened when I started to do it again and again, he began to try, and he then picked up all these things into his routine. He was not forced by me to do it but inspired and impacted by me. Most importantly, he feels respect instead of enforcement.

It applies the same in our workplace. In the initial year of my leadership, I expected my team to do things my way, and it was too much time and energy-consuming. The worst part is that I wasted their unique talents. After I changed my perspective, I always ran great teams and dug out the best from each of them differently. It's an art to own a team. It's like a head with bodies, hands, and feet. The head is the leader who gives instructions, but the head doesn't do hands and feet work. Each of them has its strength, but they look different. That makes a functional body.

So yes, a significant relationship builds up on 'change not the others, but 'change' ourselves how we do and say things, to be the impacts and inspirations. That would help people become better versions of themselves and make a win-win outcome.

Connecting before correcting. – I always put myself in a judge role and think everything must be reasonable and under my control. So I would point out the problem whenever I saw it. Isn't that familiar to you as well?

My life experience and work experience have taught me so well with bad lessons if I point out that people are wrong straight away. Everyone needs face (save their self-esteem). It took me so long to understand the magic power of connecting before correcting.

In the workplace, if I connected with my team members first and pointed out a few things they would do better, they would be willing to take my advice without being offended because there's already a strong relationship power and connection. If I don't, they can be distraught, and they will also start to count my problems and mistakes. I would appreciate and admire the good things they do first, then mention something that we could look at to improve.

A long time ago, I got a team member who resigned very suddenly to me, and I didn't know why because I did have a great attitude and conversation with her. Later, I realized that most of my conversations were about her work excellence and my expectations of her instead of connecting with her genuinely and knowing her earlier before it was too late. Connecting before correcting becomes a magical method in all relationships I deal with. My life became so much better when I used it.

In the family, it would be a disaster to correct any of my daughters without connecting with her first. She would feel so upset, and all she feels is that I don't love her and she wasn't good enough. Each time when correct after connection, I will then be a fairy-tale – a happy ending. What a supernature, humanity!

It is the same for marriage. If you start to say unique words like you are fantastic, I love you, and you are good at what you do. Then you can add a few things after, and you know the magical 'But…' Yes, if you first give advice or try to correct them. They are more likely to shut their years and feel offended instead. I tried, and it worked 99.9%, with 1% of failure because I hadn't given them enough time to connect, and I thought they were ready, so the final result might not be that perfect. It is always about progress, not perfection.

A great leader knows how not to be offendable. They are calm; they know how to respond to harsh words or embarrassing situations. Feeling offendable is widespread because we all have eagles in us, and the eagle is our pride. It is tough to accept criticism, but effortless to get compliments. Admit it or not, nowadays, more and more people would rather keep a friend who always says yes to what he asks and says good things than someone who offers criticism. When people feel judged, the very first thing they want to do is to shut the connection door quickly so that they can protect their pride.

However, the more mature I became, the more I realized that I would lose so many opportunities to grow if I only had people praising me. Why? Because most conflicts and fights come from people close to us, like our families, such as parents, siblings, children, husband, or wife. I found they were the ones who could hurt us the most. Because they are whom we spend the most time with, they know our eagles and weakness the most. No matter how beautiful the reasons behind it are for them to tell us the truth, it will become a disaster if it hurts our eagles and feelings.

It is never easy to accept the ugly truth. A fact can hurt our emotions, but if we never knew the truth, we would never be able to change for the better. As a leader in your life, if you choose to be extraordinary, to lead your own life, you must always get ready for the 'ugly truth' and 'hurting your feelings.' Because if you don't, you are just an ordinary person. Remember, you are a leader in your life; you are the decision-maker. You have the authority to choose to follow your feelings ONLY or follow the truth.

I am not a perfect leader, but I aim to be better each day with all decisions I must make every day and through my experience. The experience does not come alone by myself. It came with the people with whom I worked together.

When I started being a manager, I remember it was like a mum who had no instruction books or mentorship for raising her first kid. I always went with the bossy way because I used to believe that being a head meant the head must make all decisions, so I must be firm and harsh. I could also go blind and shut my ears because I wanted to keep my pride and authority.

Once, I faced a challenging problem, and I couldn't go anywhere when one team member asked me about the solutions. Suddenly I realized that she seemed to hold her words and was afraid to give her suggestion because of fear. She was worried that she would make me look bad or lose her job. Like an awakening call, I started to ask her suggestion, and I promised that no matter what advice she gave, the responsibility was mine. To encourage her to be bored. She gave her opinion, and I thought that was brilliant. I was thrilled.

From then on, I became the most diminutive offendable leader in my workplace. That's one of the best decisions I ever made. I changed from a 'smart' leader to a 'wise' one. I am not asking you to embrace more friends who constantly bring negative thoughts and judge you. But sometimes, if you allow moments from good people around you with different voices, you can see things differently.

It may not be pleasant initially, but once you know what you are facing is supposed to happen FOR you, not AGAINST you, your life will go to another level! We need to stay alerted to people with bad intentions, but most of the time, the words we choose to ignore are from people close to us. We tend to build up a fortress to protect our pride. We would have learned so much more if we were always open to different voices and not quickly judging or taking things personally.

If you want to be a joyful leader in life, you need to know what and why people take offense. A mature leader is a mentor to his/her team. Good leaders have strong emotional management skills.

We are living in a challenging world. In our society, there will be arrogant people who look down upon you. There will be impolite people who don't like you and treat you in nasty ways. There will be people who treat others better than you just because they don't think you deserve their respect. There will also be people who constantly take advantage of you and treat you at lower levels than them. I faced these before, and it is never a pleasant journey.

Have you been feeling and talking to yourself like this lately?

I am the mistake; (When you make a mistake)

I am not enough, and I am just not good enough; (When people don't say positive comments about you and when they care more about others than you.)

Nobody cares about me because I am not important to them; (When people don't respond or reply.)

My life is just a mess; (When someone seems to have a perfect life.)

I am not likable. (When somebody doesn't like you.)

I am useless. (When you can't do something.)

I will never be able to do it. (When you tried something many many times, you still failed.)

I have experienced all these thoughts in my mind! It's excruciating! But I Don't want to choose to listen to the **lies** above, and I prefer to listen to the **truth** below**:**

When I make a mistake, I learn from the error, and I am a better me because of learning from this mistake; there's no failure, only learning.

When I don't hear any positive feedback or comments from others just because "no news means good news" & "Bad news spreads quickly!"

When people don't contact me, I can get them when I want to because I know that everyone's life is so busy, and a true friendship lasts not based on the overall quality of time but the quality of time.

When someone else seems to have a perfect life, good on them, but only fools believe that anyone could have a problem-free life. Everyone has messes that others can't see. But the key to a "close to perfect "life is not to compare with others!

When someone doesn't like me, it's their problem and freedom, not mine. The good news is that I have more space and time for those who love me!

When I can't do one thing, I can do others because everyone has unique talents and gifts. A police officer doesn't have to know how to operate a patient, right? We are all good at something, but we can always find others to help with the things they are better at.

When I tried something many times but couldn't make it, if it's my 100th time, I still have a chance to try. What if I am thriving for the 101st time? What a waste if I give up now!

No matter how positive and bright we are, we are all constantly attacked by negative thoughts and voices in our minds. My point is, don't let our enemy -our negative thoughts ruin us! Instead, let our good thoughts speak louder and take the lead.

Do something meaningful today, and be thankful! Let our gratitude flood into our hearts and minds! Leave no room for any wrong thoughts! Life is not about pursuing no problem, but how we will respond to the problems. Or how we should treat problems as opportunities. Whatever we believe is whatever will happen! Believe something good today. Call someone today and tell them how good and important they are to you because everyone needs to hear this.

It is tough **to adjust emotions if we don't know how to practice our not-offended muscles.** We face too many things daily; 8 or 9 out of 10 are challenging. In other words, they are hard rather than easy. When I realized the truth of life, I concluded three enemies, and then I practiced avoiding these lacks to help me build up my offense-free muscles.

Let's find out why we are offended. What are the enemies who are making us angry? I found them for you, my friend. I found them because I had suffered from all of these pain before, and since I found them and acknowledged them, I could then deal with them. I could still be offended, but not that quickly and easily offended for no reason anymore, as I found all the answers and started practicing my not-offended muscles every day.

Enemy number one: 'Lacks.'
Why are we easy to get angry sometimes? We need to be aware of our emotions and listen to ourselves to find out why and then take our first step to action. These are situations when I could lose my temper or become frustrated. I concluded the causes to be 'Lacks. 'Yes, 'Lacks' are the main reasons we lose our tempers or self-control. So, to train our not-offended muscles, the first step is to avoid the 'lack' and feed your 'lack' to full. Like your car, if you don't refuel it, it will run out of fuel and lose its function. Keep refuelling to fill your 'lacks.' Let me reveal to you the **LACKS**!!

1.   Lack of sleep or rest.
When I am too tired, and if I don't have enough sleep, my physical mind and body can't function 100%, I feel helpless, and I get easy to be angry or impatient. Sleep is one of the most magical medicines I could find. I don't know about you, but after a good sleep, the world again becomes a heavenly place to me. But if I lack sleep, sometimes it can feel like hell. Even physical or mental uncomfortableness can go away quickly when I sleep well. The benefits of sleep are massive. You can do any research to find more answers.

Are you offended easily recently? Are you easily angry? First, give yourself a quick self-check: Are you sleeping too late lately? Do you wake up too early? Do you need to improve your sleep quality? When was the last time you seriously had a good rest? Without overthinking or worrying about your work, family issues, chaos, or anything? Just have a peaceful mind? After all, 'sleep' is one of the most activities everyone on earth does. I have found some great ways to help me sleep better, but everyone has their tailored, magical way of having a great sleep.

When I started my company, at the initial 2-3 months, I didn't realize that I was almost 7-24hours thinking of the business and trying to make it run well. But one day, I finally crushed down, and I started to be so angry and impatient with things for no reason. I began to sit down and re-look at my schedule, and little did I realize I was planning almost meetings every night, and I got zero plans for rest.

To avoid being offended, we must start by preventing the Lack of sleep or rest. So, I put rest to my schedule as one essential to-do list too. That helped so much.

Here is some scientific research about sleep. It is fascinating.

54 Shocking Sleep Statistics, Data, and Trends Revealed for 2022 (sleepadvisor.org)

Link: https://www.sleepadvisor.org/sleep-statistics/

It says: "In just 10 minutes, these 54 sleep statistics will make it clear that sleeping disorders and deprivation are NO JOKE, and we should all take our sleep more seriously. Knowing all this might save your or someone's life."

It also says: "Not getting enough sleep may cause problems with learning, reacting, and focusing, making it difficult to make decisions, control your emotions, solve problems, or cope with change."

Please have a read about it.

2. Lack of progress or growth

I will lose my joy when I am not making progress and living my life repeatedly with nothing new, no breakthrough. That's when we may become offensive again. It does not often happen now because I constantly seek opportunities to grow and progress with small things. All the little efforts I made before made me today, and all the little steps I am making now will make the future me.

I remember that when I married Luke and lived in Hong Kong, my work was at its peak as it was so successful with good pay and easy for me to handle because I was so good at what I was doing. The company was flourishing too. We got Luke's family to prepare dinner for us, and every day I went to work, came home with dinner ready, and spent a bit of family time; after that, it was another day. Sometimes we could go out to eat expensive food together as a family. Life seemed to be great, but one day, I realized something was missing, and that was a joy. I couldn't make much progress in my life, so I couldn't find much more passion. One day, I was unusually angry for nothing; later, I realized it was simply because I wanted to make more progress and growth.

Then I started to source new things to learn; I went to the Spanish evening school and found different subjects to grow my knowledge. My no-offended muscles began to come back. A great lesson learned to realize that stopping growth will also take my joy away because of no fulfillment.

3. Lack of faith

What do you believe? Whom do you trust? When things are not going as expected, you can be easily offended or discouraged if you don't believe in it. People could only show dedication easily if they had a pleasant experience or tried it before.

Knowing that your anxiety can take your joy away if you lack faith is essential. It is one of the biggest enemies you face in life. You will read from one of the following chapters about finding your faith to conquer your fear. However, hold on to your faith and not just rely on yourself if you are a believer. If you are not a believer in any religion, find one. My faith in Christianity transformed my life. I can live a refreshing life with confidence every single day. I'd love to share my Christian faith journey in another book one day. My life with faith has completely transformed me and made my life whole.

In the bible, Hebrews 11:1 says: "Now faith is the assurance of things hoped for, the conviction of things not seen."

People's true stories are compelling. I suggest you read this article about Christian celebrities and what they said in 2020.

Link: https://premierchristian.news/en/news/article/faith-of-the-famous-christian-celebrities-and-what-they-said-in-2020

Here are some Christian celebrities they mentioned:

<u>Justin Bieber</u>
<u>Mark Zuckerberg</u>
<u>Tyson Fury</u>
<u>Stormzy</u>
<u>Chris Pratt</u>
<u>Letitia Wright</u>
<u>Billy Vunipola</u>
<u>Robbie Williams</u>
<u>Roberto Firmino</u>
<u>Mark Wahlberg</u>
<u>Matthew McConaughey</u>
<u>Angel Gomes</u>
<u>Kayne West</u>

The common thing about them is that they give glory and credit to God, not themselves, and because of faith, they do not need to rely purely on themselves. Human has a limit, but God doesn't. Yes, we always have something more spiritual that is much bigger than ourselves.

Start to find your faith journey today, you will start a new life that is no longer alone, and you will meet the best version of yourself on another level.

4. Lack of self-care

You can't be strong all day and undefeatable without a healthy body. Therefore, so many sick people will most likely be depressed. Because they found they are helpless and they are weak.

I insist on doing my hair and nails regularly, and I have specific rules in life that I will abide by to ensure I feel good. During the most extended lockdown in Melbourne, when most people wore PJs at work and did not switch on their cameras, I remained to be myself. I changed myself to be from office mode to housewife and mum roles. Even though I was home for 24 hours, I insisted on exercising and never stopped. It made me feel fantastic and ready for any daily battles or challenges. I always turned on my camera for video conferences; I had face-to-face meetings virtually with people every day.

My self-care helped me to be calm and more helpful to others too. I felt great, and I could always make some colleagues laugh during the hard time when so many people were suffering from mental health. I never lost my purpose, even though we were all facing setbacks and were feeling stuck. I enjoyed it a lot, and I had to be thankful for my efforts in self-care.

Not everyone was as on the track as me, and people started to lose intention and purpose when they no longer wanted to make much effort in their self-care. My mum was a typical example. The version I knew six years ago still cared about her dress and outlook, she loved buying new clothes, and the small things made her happy. Her passion for life was no longer there. Don't get me wrong, and we don't need to spend hours making ourselves look better, but 20 minutes a day is necessary. I remember that when my mum lost her intention of looking after herself, she started to get no interest in anything, lost her passion, and began to lose her identity too. She got anxious or angry much more straightforwardly, which is not the mum I knew before.

If we don't look after ourselves, how can we look after others around us? We need to be careful that, as leaders, we are leading an example. If we show a bad example, our followers will learn bad things, so our standards are essential. We use the example of safety instructions of airplanes about the mask dropped off that we should do it for ourselves first to help others. It is not to tell us how to be selfish but to let us know that an unselfish person will care for himself and others. Because if you need to care for others, you must ensure you have a healthy body to manage.

I always joke with my hubby when he gains weight again. I said,

"Don't be so selfish. Take care of yourself, ok? We all need you; if you are sick, we must take care of you too." Sounds mean, right? But it is true that if you don't take care of yourself, you bring more trouble and burdens to others. That's why I always try to manage myself not to be sick and not to give loads to my family.

If you take care of yourself well, your tolerance of negative things or languages will become much more substantial. You can fight more battles. You won't need to seek more respect and expect others to feed you to feel better. We are often offended or angry because people's answers differ from our expectations.

Now you know the LACKS that you can check back whenever you get offended. Instead of being angry and focusing on what others did was wrong, if you focus on filling all the lacks of gaps, there's no hole or crack the enemy could get into you.

Enemy Number Two: Jealousy/Comparison – It kills your joy.
Do you ever have the moment when you are so happy with what you have, but suddenly, someone appears in your life, and it seems that they have everything better than you? Do you feel like your life worsens in one day after comparing it with that person? Do you ever check someone's social media and feel like your life is a mess compared to that person's perfect life?

Here are the things about the comparison. We must understand that we are naturally competitive and will always have the first thought when seeing someone good, but what makes us different is how we choose to respond after competitive reviews.

We can choose to be jealous and keep competing with others, or we can choose to be happy for others, then quickly switch back to our lives and stay in our movie cast. Don't live in others' movies and shows because you will only play a supporting role in others' lives. Only playing on track in your film can make you the Protagonist.

Here is one vital thing to everyone living in the 21st century and afterward. If we don't change how we use social media, we will all be used by social media. Believe it or not, the joy of our life will only become less.

The danger of social media:
Warning!!
You must know at least five kinds of danger when you check social media too often.

1. *It can quickly drive you to a negative side, make you offended and stressed out (sometimes what people were trying to say wasn't what your understandings were, this is the problem about a social media post with a one-way voice.)*
2. *It creates a distraction that can cause you to lose direction and focus.*
3. *It can unconsciously drive you to a comparable mode and make you feel your life isn't as good.*
4. *It drives your unrealistic expectations and energy to perfectionism when the things or people you see are perfect on social media, while our real life isn't perfect. A reasonable expectation is critical to your response and changes your joy level.*
5. *It kills so much of your time and energy that you lose real-life time with real people and essential stuff.*

Since we cannot hide from the real world and its high technology, let's do these instead:

✅ **Always read posts neutrally. See things from different angles. Don't apply everything to yourself because everyone is different.**

- ✅ Spend more time working on improving yourself through any aspect rather than holding your phone for no reason.
- ✅ Strictly limit your time on social media. Allow purposely looking for specific things you need ONLY!
- ✅ For friends and families in real life, if there's anything you can say in person or by phone, do these instead of commenting only on the posts.
- ✅ For friends or families overseas, it's good to post and keep memories but don't treat social media as more critical or prioritized than honest conversation and communication.
- ✅ Focus on being the director and star in your movie! That's the only way to make your movie successful.

I love social media because it is so convenient, and I post a lot for family memories (I also need to be aware of online safety.) I only go around and check others' posts for a few minutes. There were some days I found I was super distracted. One hour flew by while I was holding my phone, and I felt so offended. That's when I decided to avoid unnecessary phone time intentionally.

A real friend will always be there for you, even though you may chat or meet occasionally. I appreciate whoever is reading my post and has greatly supported the social media channel in my journey. Kind encouragement is important and influential in people's lives, so let's keep being these people to make a difference in this world by using this channel, not other harmful things! Expect social media life to be something different than real life. We must adjust our expectations because they are 'FAKE' more than 'TRUE.' It's always better to spend time with real friends than on social media. After all, our life is too short to live in a fantasy.

A real friend is a true friend. **A true friend will be with you, whether you are in a higher or lower position.** There's a reason why some of our best friends always come from school time. Because when we were at school, things were less commercial. It's pure friendship. Society builds up a trend that people get close to you for some 'gaining intention.' 'Intention' to get things from you. A fake friend will only appear when you are in good time, and they disappear when you need help.

A real friend will be around not because you are perfect but because you are imperfect and make mistakes, but you are YOU. They won't just say good things to you; they **do** good things for you too. A good deed is more authentic than a good saying. Find your real friend today. Do not waste your time on social media to be friends with 1 million fake ones who won't even be around you when you need someone. Cherish the one who delivers you food when you are hungry and calls you to encourage you when you are down. *One true friend is better than one million fake ones.*

Remember that you are the authentic leader of your life. Your life is real. Let's live in the real one! Let technology serve us, not control, and lead us! Please don't live in other people's lives and be busy being their audience. It is your time to be the protagonist and director in your movie!

Enemy Number Three: Wrong Perspective / Wrong Expectations
Nobody could offend you unless you decide to be offended.
We must change our perspective when something happens. When someone was rude to me, here is the fundamental perspective I need to hold firmly: What people are doing reflects them. & People got their own problems to fix.

If I am not feeling complete or if something is missing, I tend to complain and seek from outside of my body. Conversely, if I am feeling great and nothing is lacking inside of me and feeling grateful, nobody can make me angry. Thus, I choose not to hand over my joy to others to control. **I decide not to be the victim or the leader of my emotion.**

Why do I say that? Whenever I am treated disrespectfully, I will first acknowledge that this guy has his issues and they are not feeling complete. Like every one of you, I have two choices. Choice one: be mad or say something horrible back. It will ruin my peace, self-control, and joy, and it simply means that I was willing to hand over my happiness to somebody else and hurt them simultaneously. It will create a lose-lose cycle.

Or choose two, let them do what they do, and stay away from them, but I won't take what they say personally. What awful things they are saying are reflected in what they are lacking. Or, if their words were meaningful and factual, it would be a perfect chance for me to learn and improve instead of feeling offended. One of my life goals is always win-win. To ignore a person's rudeness doesn't mean I am weak; it simply means that I am the leader. I take control of my emotions and my situation.

Why can't we be the leaders of our emotions and thoughts? You don't have control over what the outside may bring to you, but you have 100% control over every conversation and how it will end up.

Don't EVER feel that you are the victim, don't ever feel that your pain is the most compared to anyone in the world! Because it is never true!

The truth is: there will always be someone in the world who is pitier than you! Who is suffering more than you, but it is never what the outside world chooses to let you down; it is your thought and choice! The choice that enables you to feel you are the victim! You never know how strong you can become if you believe you are a victim!! You will only become who you think you are!

Don't get me wrong. It doesn't mean that you didn't suffer, and it doesn't mean that others have no fault. But you must believe **that everything happens for a beautiful reason!** Yes, **believe that things are happening for you, not against you!** Maybe it is the thing that happened that you broke up with someone, rather than feeling that you are not good enough, it is the time for you to believe and prepare somebody much better for you! Rejection is always a redirection to something better! Maybe someone was so mean to you, and you are judged by people you love all the time; rather than feeling that you are vulnerable, it is the time for you to get stronger, to prepare for more enormous challenges in your life so that you can achieve more!

Maybe you lost your loved ones in your life. Rather than dwelling in the past forever, it is the time to remind yourself to move on and be more grateful that you shall cherish more with those still alive. If you don't clear the space to receive new things, you will only remain in the past.

Why is leading your thought so important? Because it can completely change your mind and perspective. Do you want to lead a good or bad life? Your choice!

I always use the 'looking at one & two' strategy to keep my life positive.

Rule Number One: Knowing your 1 & 2
Good or Bad! I choose to focus on the big 1 & 2, which is the only way to enjoy my life.

My childhood life wasn't that good with what I had to experience, but I still ended up thriving and being joyful and different despite what my experienced old life was trying to make me. Yes, when I looked at the good side of my life, the wrong sides started to fade. It doesn't mean that the bad side doesn't exist. It simply means my mind is too busy to focus on the good side and infilling the good things, so there is no more room or space for the wrong or negative things.

When I say: focus on the 1 & 2, I mean that our life is full of trouble and problems, and our life is hard. If we put 10 out of 10 as our life, probably 8 to 9 seem to be bad parts or sad parts, but don't forget that we still have the 1 & 2 left for good. That's what people call positive thoughts. I am well-known as a very positive person. It doesn't mean that I am anger free or I am trying to be pretending positively. The ultimate reason is that I do not want to choose to be miserable and dwell on the uncontrollable hostile environment or situations if I can't change them for the time being. I believe there's always magic to looking at the other side of things, which is to be positive and look at the 1 & 2.

Why is it so important to focus on the 1 & 2? Because what you are focusing on is what you are going to get. My 8-year-old daughter once woke up at 5 am, crying and saying that she was scared of the darkness, but the funny thing was she had been sleeping alone in her room for so long, and she didn't feel scared anymore. I said to my daughter: Your environment is the same, where you have been sleeping by yourself for the last few years, so why are you afraid? It would be best if you trusted that you were safe.

Many people in the world always think that they are the products of the environment. The environment produced them, but wait a minute, if that's the case, why suddenly, in the same environment, could my daughter have been afraid? Yes, it is her mind and her thought, and it is her focus that when she is focusing on the darkness and something unknown or she starts to imagine any horrible things which do not exist, she could make up her mind, and then her mind will tell her she is scared. It is not the environment but our focus. What we are focusing on is what we are going to get.

I used to fear the darkness a lot, and there were so many nights when I lived in my hometown without any streetlights. I had to run and run each time I came home late, and every time it was like a disaster film. I was like the main character in Jurassic World, and I had to run and run, being so scared, but from nothing, but a deep unknown fear, which is just something in my mind that I made up and focused on. After hundreds of times of practice and I felt exhausted, and then I realized that only if I changed my focus to something else I immediately feel unafraid anymore. So, whenever I had to walk in the darkness, I would focus on beautiful things or anything that could give me peace, calm, or joy; I would feel so safe and enjoyable because what I choose to focus on is what I am going to get.

Recently we had a trip with a friend's family. The story is real, but I changed the person's name to keep privacy. So, Jolin is the wife, and Sam is the husband. They have two kids just like us. During the trip, I found it weird that Jolin is always the one who drives, as I know most of the time, women would prefer a man to drive, just like me, who would always prefer my hubby to drive. Even if one person drives, the other should be able to take turns, especially with a long-time drive. So, I asked why she had to drive, and Sam never took his turn. The fascinating answer is that Jolin discovered that she would not feel car sick if she could drive. That is fascinating and very truly reflects our real life.

When she focuses on driving, her mind is filled with thoughts like 'how to drive well,' 'where next,' 'How to be safe,' and so on. It needs lots of concentration, so she has no time or attention to feel car sick. Isn't that so true for our life?

The other story is from Peter Sage, an inspirational speaker who wrote a very influential book called 'Mud or Star.' The book he wrote when he was in prison changed hundreds to thousands of people's life in prison. It was about two men in jail that one man only sees the mud, and he complains all day, but the other man only sees the star outside the window, and he feels great all the time. That story helped hundreds and thousands of people from committing suicide and allowed them to change and believe in life again. They got rid of drugs as well. It is s powerful and influential when we look at things from different perspectives.

Rule Number Two: Find your 1&2
Here is something I found when I looked at the big 1 & 2; I could feel so joyful even though something terrible could have happened to me.

If you feel the worst day you suffered at work, you still have a job! Many people have capabilities but don't have opportunities! If you are feeling the worst day ever in your life, you still have a life!

How Many People Die Each Day https://worldpopulationreview.com/countries/deaths-per-day

> **World Death Rate**
> **Deaths**
> **per Day:**166,279**Deaths**
> **per Hour:**6,928**Deaths**
> **per Minute:**115 **Deaths**
> **per Second:**1.92

If you are sick and it seems nobody understands or cares how you are feeling, think about many people are dying and are rarely known by anyone. You still have someone in your world that you can cherish and should be grateful for.

If you are stressed about your financial situation, there are homeless people and people who struggle for their daily food. You still have food and a place to live. With your values, you can always find any ways to make a living! There are 663 million undernourished people, and they could die anytime without food. https://ourworldindata.org/hunger-and-undernourishment

If you have painful arms or legs, look around: many people have no more arms or legs and wish they could have these feelings again. Or it is to remind you that it is time to take care of your physical body. Rather than feeling sorry for yourself, why not celebrate that you still have an entire body?

Did you ever hear many stories about someone who used to complain that they had too much hair, then one day, they lost hair because of a specific disease and had to find ways to grow it back? Do you know, every day, so many people in the world lose their legs, arms, hands, or normal abilities because of accidents, and some lose their family, house, or everything, and they start to struggle with everything?

In short, we live in different seasons, and each season can change quickly. Rather than complaining about the rain, why not enjoy the rainbow after the rain before it disappears? Rather than complaining about the snow, why not build a snowman that melts before the snow gets melted? Rather than complaining about the sun, why not enjoy the sunshine before the rain comes? So, looking at your 1 & 2 is very powerful and brings you more gratitude. Only a grateful person can be joyful.

Rule Number 3: Counting your 8 & 9.
To look at 1 & 2 is to be grateful and selfless. But wait, is it true 1 & 2? Or is it how we feel that we only have 1 & 2?

Here is what I found in my life: When you are very focused on your life, and you have a great blueprint and perfect expectations for everything, you may find: Why things cannot go as smoothly as you expected and as well as how you planned? Therefore, you may feel so hard to deal with the situation because dealing with smooth things is easy as it does not cost any of your energy. Instead, it allows you to enjoy it supernaturally, and if it is the hard thing, your first institutional mind will feel sick about it and want to avoid that situation unless you take the lead and face it and have strong faith in dealing with it.

1 & 2 is when you intentionally start to count your blessings and appreciate little things in life. Break down your life into small gratefulness, you can find 8 to 9, and then your big troubles start to fade away from your mind or shrink because your energy goes mainly to gratitude,

and being grateful is to appreciate the little things in life. It is the most effective way to find your joy every single day.

Prove it? Try to do this.

Sit down and find a peaceful and quiet place without distractions if you have recently been overwhelmed or depressed. Just do this and tell me how you feel after.

Bring a pen and a notebook, or you can even use a phone or computer, but you have to ensure there isn't a distraction. A pen and a notebook will be the most effective option.

Now, let yourself list your worries and the overwhelming things you think you are facing, things as Money worries, Work/Career worries, whatever. Then on the other page of your notebook, write down every little thing you can count as a blessing. Such as you have a bed to sleep in, a family, a pen to write to, a house to live in, a healthy body for now, or anything.

Please also do the same thing for any person in your family you are facing relationship challenges. Are you frequently fighting with your husband, wife, kids, or colleague? On one page, you write down things you don't like or their problems; on the other page, you write down things you admire or their strength.

How about you do it also for yourself? Write down the things you don't think you are bad at about yourself, then list those you are capable of. Don't forget, to count blessings means you have to trust every single thing on this list. Things like any small kindness you had to people or any small achievement you had before (I believe it must be a lot if you start to look for them.)

Once you have done it, you will find the outcome and result. That will explain why I asked you to count you 8 & 9. Because we truly have more joy and gratefulness than trouble. Everyone truly has more things people could appreciate and admire than 'being hated.' Complaining will only make bad things exaggerated, enlarge your problem, and increase negativities.

Being positive doesn't mean you are fake and doing things that aren't true or against your feelings, but to turn down the negativities because they are supposed to be the 1&2, but they always make you believe that they are the more significant portion 8 & 9.

Start to count your actual 8 & 9 today. **Count your blessings, gratefulness, the good part, and things you have rather than what you don't have.**

A joyful leader is the most charming leader that every follower would love to follow! We know who we are and how to love ourselves completely, but how can we count our blessings if we have a heavy burden on us? Do we still have the capacity or energy to count our blessings? No, we don't. That is why we must learn how to break the chain of our past to let it go.

CHAPTER FOUR

Clear joyful leadership barrier.

Lead to let it go.

Things that happened are gone! Dwelling in the past is completely wasting your time!!

Time is not money! Time is life! You can earn more money, but you can never get more time. You can only prioritize your time. Every minute of your time is part of your life; you have a better choice to live every minute of it or waste it completely!!

If you want to lead your life, you must start with leading to break the chain of your past. If you are too weary and with too many shadows of your past in you, you cannot be a great leader for your future or anybody else's future.

Here are two research talking about bad leadership:

One: The Worst Boss Behaviours
https://www.bamboohr.com/blog/bad-boss-index-the-worst-boss-behaviors-according-to-employees-infographic

Two: The top 10 bad leadership behaviours
https://www.bamboohr.com/blog/top-bad-leadership-behaviors-how-to-avoid

During this research, it mentioned ten bad behaviours of a leader.

1. Takes credit for employees' work
2. Lacks trust in employees
3. Overworks people
4. Refuses to advocate for employees' compensation
5. Hires or promotes the wrong people
6. Shifts blame in disputes between employees and clients
7. Fails to provide direction
8. Micromanages
9. Focuses on employees' weaknesses more than their strengths
10. Fails to set clear expectations

Why do these people even do that? If it's not because the guy lacks security or faith, there must be something else. And here comes constructive research about how the trauma from your past (childhood) could affect you.

Seven hidden ways childhood trauma affects you as an adult:
https://www.powerofpositivity.com/7-hidden-ways-childhood-trauma-affects-you-as-an-adult/

It talked about:

Anxiety and Depression
Substance Abuse
Social Difficulties
Health Problems

Kristy Guo

Lost Opportunities
Low Self-Esteem
Lack of Direction

Don't underestimate what your childhood and past could do to your future. I suffered in my childhood, with many painful times and memories. These taught me more about life. It made me feel sorry whenever I saw someone who might have suffered the same thing. You will be surprised at how many times I could cry when I watched anything emotional or touching. I don't cry much in real life, but I cry a lot on listening to others' stories. Even though we know movies and films are fiction, emotions are real.

I felt I was not good enough a long time ago. I once felt like going away from my family and never wanted to go back home anymore, and I even started to plan how to leave and where to go.

Here is a bit of background story: my parents raised me, and my grandparents raised my sister. The good thing about being with my parents was that I still had parents. But everything else seemed to be a disaster. Seeing domestic violence was one thing. Not being taken care of properly is another thing. I constantly felt that I was like an orphan. Back then, all my parents' thoughts were to work and get enough money to support the family. There was no standard for parenting. Like probably some other families in the same generation, especially in our hometown in China, our parents didn't and wouldn't intentionally spend much time with their children. It was why I couldn't have much conversation with them, and I felt so lonely and ignored.

Looking back, I think my sister also felt like the victim as she didn't understand why our grandparents raised her and why couldn't she be chosen to stay with her parents and sister. However, her life to me was much better in my childhood. At least she had her grandparents' care every day. She often got new clothes, and I always had to wear old ones. She would have special treats on her table from our grandparents because they raised her. It made my heart ache every time. I was too young to understand 'comparison is a joy killer' and 'my sister had her pain too.'

I didn't understand why we both were their grandkids and why they treated us so differently. I was so upset for many times, and Mum always asked me to hold my anger or sadness, and just behave to be a good girl. I had to wipe my tears and pretend it was OK. One of my aunties always teased me and said: "You were probably the adopted kid in this family." I was too little to understand her joke, so my heart was sore whenever I was mistreated. Deep in my heart, I thought I wasn't good enough and didn't deserve a better life.

I had three choices: to escape and do the silly things that I thought to leave my family, but that could probably bring me to a worse situation. I could be sold, sexually abused, or killed by anybody. Two, I could hold my anger and jealousy in me and keep allowing them to attack my feelings and emotions daily. But I was too hungry to be happy, so I chose the third choice, 'let it go.' Because only letting it go can bring me all the joy and sweetness in life again.

Never make decisions when you are angry because you will make bad choices. Like my story, I slowly understood that how my grandparents treated my sister didn't mean they didn't love me. It simply means they knew more about my sister's demands and wanted to give her more. I started to look at the brighter side of it. I began to choose to remember those good times I had with my grandparents. That taught me that life *could be unfair, but if you let it go and move on, things will be OK. Until one day, you will understand why. Tell yourself that you choose to be an extraordinary person who can love and forgive.*

There are many people in my life that I can judge based on what I see, their inappropriate behaviours, or poor life outcome. Remember one of the stories that I got bullied during school, and once when I was 12, I travelled alone. When I took a train back to school, a rude guy threw me to the ground just because I fell asleep after taking a long-distance journey without a seat. I was too tired, he was so rough, and I felt that was one of my worst days ever. I thought I was not enough, not worthy, and more negative feelings could have attacked me. I suffered domestic violence in my family when I was little, and many of the years of my life were filled with tears and horror just because my Dad was an alcoholic and hit my Mum all the time a long-time ago.

Being successful before doesn't mean you are successful now, nor will you be successful in the future because of your past! What you are today isn't because of your past, but you chose to use your past as your definition to be where you are and who you are today!

Break the chain of your past! It is never too late because we don't live in the past. We live now for the future! Make a choice now! Be your leader, and choose to focus on where you want to be in the future! If you want to have a particular life, imagine it, then go and live for it!! It may take faster or slower, but you will get there! There is nothing that can stop you except for yourself!

Imagine you are stuck in the forest, and you know there can be dangers in the woods, and there might be dangerous animals in front of you on the way out. Will you give up trying and waiting for death, or will you figure out ways to escape?

Break the chain from the past that holds you back!

Break the chain from the past that is telling you that you are successful enough and there is no need to make more effort. That's not true! **Our life is a journey, not a destination!**

Break the chain from the past that is telling you that you are not good enough with all your experiences and background! That can never hold you back unless you believe it!

My childhood memories could have been a deep scar for me to

dwell in and never come out, but I was grateful and magnified the good, which helped to shrink the bad! The suffering and pains made me much firmer to fight and make efforts to achieve what I wanted and where I wanted to be!

I am still growing and learning because our life is supposed to be dancing in the storm, singing in pain! Wherever we choose to look is wherever we want to be!

Do you want to have a better life? Then don't look at the past and live in the past; look at now and live in now.

Do you want to find happiness in your life? Then look at the joy now, not happy when!

One of the Holy Bible, Luke 6:37, says: **"Forgive then you shall be forgiven."** That's right. **To forgive others is to forgive yourself. It is not for the others' good, but more for your own good.** *Unforgiving one person takes long-lasting time and energy but forgiving someone only takes one decision.*

We mix 'forgive' and 'forget.' So, when we say I will forgive that person, we force ourselves to forget what happened. But the fact is nobody can force us to forget. The more we force ourselves to forget, the more we shall remember, and probably the pain will hide deeper in some dark corner where you are not even aware anymore. But now and then, the pain will come and bother you, impacting your behaviour.

I was heartbroken by my Dad's behaviour toward Mum and his careless and irresponsible role as a father for a long time. Although I always tried to be positive, forgive, and forget, the negative feeling would bother me again after a while and may still upset me. It's not easy or probably impossible for me to let go of them all, but there's no better way than to let go.

I remember once I had to go back to my hometown after almost ten years, and it was a long way. It needed the current fast transportation. I had to go alone; it had been years since I lived in my hometown (a small town in China). It was hazardous because it was almost close to midnight, and there were few people you could ask for help. There were a few stops I had to transfer to reach the destination. Long story short, transporting the last station became a business of monopolization. It was all taken by a group of people who drive taxis. In other words, you could go nowhere if you don't use their services.

There was this guy who looked so abusive and dangerous, and I was so nervous and scared because there were many bad stories I had heard about people being robbed or harmed by illegal taxi drivers. I had to pretend to call my family, while when I was calling, my Dad was the only one in my hometown who was the closest one I could get help from, as my Mum went to my sister's overseas and wasn't there. I remember I was so worried; my heartbeat was fast, my body was shaking, and I sincerely asked my Dad if he could help to send someone to get me, but he said no, I couldn't, and he said he was busy gambling (playing Pokka cards.) I was so upset and felt so helpless. That wasn't the first time I felt hopeless, and it trained me to be even more robust and to find a way myself. But that experience hurt me badly.

I had no better choice but to get on one of the taxis. I told the guy not to take any more passengers, and I agreed with his price, which was ridiculously high – 10 times more. I remember the original price was about RMB50, and he charged me RMB500. I wanted to reject it straight away, but when I saw so many taxi drivers only take passengers if they could get four more people so that they could make a consolidation to drop off each of them along the way. It will take four times more of my time. I just wanted to get rid of the risk soon, and it was too dangerous to get strangers sitting in the same car, and many of them were very aggressive, and anything bad could happen. So I agreed and said I would only pay when he dropped me off safely. In the meantime, I started to picture myself with Kungfu so that I could fight to protect myself, and I was highly alerting the whole way. He still got three more people into the car and broke his promise. I was so upset, but again, no better choice.

Luckily, I ended up being safe, but I had to call one of the uncles and aunties to borrow one of their spare rooms to sleep in. That night, I cried for so long. I even thought I wasn't necessary or good enough to be loved by my father, and I felt, once again, like an orphan.

There are more stories I can tell, but dwelling on the past or unforgiving, anyone has nothing good to do for us except bring a heavy burden to weigh us down. The person you decided to hate or be angry about probably doesn't even remember or care anymore. Why should we keep suffering from the time when they hurt us forever? It's ultimately a waste of our life and time. By realizing that, I had to process the healing, find ways to forgive, and truly let it go.

I didn't feel I should treat my father better because of his behaviours, but I didn't allow my emotion to ruin my life. I kept doing what I needed to support him and the family financially and spiritually. I always text him nice words to let him know I appreciate what he has done well for me and any efforts (even though sometimes I could hardly count on any.) I chose to find all the limited good memories I had with my father when I was 4 or 5, and I magnified them to show him that I believe in him for good. Because that's the only way to let him feel loved and forgiven so that he can be better and be willing to believe in himself, I know that he always feels he's broken and not a good or qualified father. But who else is perfect on earth?

Let's be honest; how could it be so easy to break the chain and forget about the past? How could it be so easy to let it go? Well, you are right, it is never easy, and it is pretty hard. But we must know that 'to let it go' is not to hide the pain in our body and use something new to cover them or pretend we are ok when we are not ok. Finding temporary comfort does not resolve the root of your problem.

What does this mean? Let me ask you some questions.

Are you the type of person who will buy new clothes or go shopping when you feel stressed? Are you the type of person who does lots of cleaning when you think life is messy? Are you the type of person who will smoke more when you have a heavy burden? Are you the type of person who will drink alcohol when you are upset? Are you the type of person who will look for comfort and confidence through social media when you are feeling down? Or are you the type of person who said: "well, I need a day off to recover!" But after doing all the best things to treat yourself, you still feel that something is missing. And the worst thing is even though you rested on the weekends or through an extended holiday, you still couldn't feel entirely energetic, motivational, or happy.

We all have multiple versions of our personalities. There are more things in our life we can list, and I am one of you for a few of the above-listed items, except that I never do smoking or turn to alcohol. I would do the rest when I was younger to make myself feel better. And I admit I did try to look for things to do that could make me feel better temperately, but I started to realize that most of the time when I want to do something to 'let it go, it wasn't really 'let it go, it became 'let it go aside,' it is a huge difference.

"Our biggest enemy is ourselves." That's right. We do have two voices in our minds all the time. That is why you need to understand more about yourself. Based on my previous experience and understanding of our emotions, I want you to know that we all need Dr. Con, and we need to know that Dr. Con and Mr. Subcon must meet each other with a good conversation. If you are suffering from a mental health issue, it is still good to find an expert to help you, but after reading this little story, I believe it will help you to know yourself more.

You will also be interested to read an article here by Robert L. Leahy Ph.D.: Are You Your Own Worst Enemy? | Psychology Today

Link: https://www.psychologytoday.com/us/blog/anxiety-files/201710/are-you-your-own-worst-enemy

It says, "Depression and anxiety are often because of the self-critical voice that defeats you before you start, robs you of any credit for anything that you do, and makes you afraid of trying anything because you fear the loathing and regret that will follow. In this post, I outline seven techniques to defeat this self-critical voice so you can feel better about being a real human being."

You have the right to decide which inner voice is the boss and whom you want to listen to. Dr. Con is the one in you that oversees your happiness, he is the doctor of your mental and spiritual health, and Mr. Subcon is the one who is in charge of your habits and first response. There are so many things Dr. Con will let go of or already forget, but Mr. Subcon will keep them somewhere in the deep of your heart and mind that become part of the reasons for how you respond and how you feel when things happen.

We all face daily suffering and pains, whether from life or work, most likely from people around us. We all need to be our own doctors for any bad things happening in life unless it is a prominent, well-known illness that we have hospitals and doctors to go to. We all know that two significant thoughts and ideas are always in our minds fighting all day. You may all be familiar with the cartoon reflected views of 'angel' and 'devil' that the angel will say things to guide you to be a good guy, and the devil will guide you to be a bad guy. No matter how many times we lie to ourselves, pretending how perfect we are. We all make good and bad decisions, and nobody has a perfect life.

It is essential to schedule a spiritual doctor's appointment for yourself. Let's imagine one mind is your conscious mind which we call Dr. Con, and meet with your subconscious mind, which we call Mr. Subcon.

Remember, Dr. Con is calm and full of wisdom and knowledge. He stays awake and thinks often; he is humble and full of self-awareness, with no sugar-coating. However, Mr. Subcon is very emotional and stubborn, and he constantly thinks he knows everything and always believes what he has been doing is the best. In short, Mr. Subcon is proud (overconfident) and over-protective but venerable, negative, and emotional. We all have Dr. Con and Mr. Subcon in us, and there's no doubt.

We have four steps when they meet that are exactly like when we see a doctor.

Step one: Search.
Your Dr. Con needs to check and diagnose the problem of Mr. Subcon and find out the spiritual illness which is the root of the problem.

Step Two: Check.
Mr. Subcon will acknowledge it.
Step three: Finding solutions
Find out what to do to let go of this disease or illness.

Step four: Provide 'Medicine'
It would be best if you had the formula or spiritual medicine to fix your mind and spiritual illness.

Here are the potential communications between them in your mind.

This needs to come through the communication between Dr. Con and Mr. Subcon. Dr. Con will ask questions like: Can you tell me what you have been suffering from recently? What is the pain you have been facing?

Mr. Subcon may say: I have been grumpy recently, and I don't know why. I feel that my life is painful when I am experiencing this again and again, I seem to need a change, but I am too lazy to change.

Dr. Con: "Can you list things that make you angry?" Then Mr. Subcon will list tons of things such as below:

- "I am always tired; overwhelmed; worried about my study, my work, and my future
- I am always angry when I see people's words are mean or rude to me
- I am always not feeling fulfilled
- I am always not feeling successful
- I don't always feel that I am enough
- I don't always feel I am good because of what I do
- And the list goes on and on."

Dr. Con: "tell me why these happen to you. What did you do or did not do?"

Mr. Subcon: 'As you know, my name is Subconscious mind, which I am famous for and proud of. I won't do much to prevent these, but here are what I do: once it is built up as a habit, it will become my power.

- I sleep late and can't find my passion, but I suppose that's life, right?
- I always think more than I do because I am intelligent and good at thinking.
- I always worry about things that I haven't done and things that haven't happened yet, because I want certainty.
- I always expect people to respect me when I show so much respect to people, you know, the feeling of expecting others to do what I think they are supposed to? Do you understand?
- I am always trying, but I don't feel fulfilled, especially when I have attempted to do more than three times, and if I am doing one thing for a few days, I have no patience to wait anymore.
- I am not feeling successful because to be successful must achieve something big! You know, like become a president? Like, become the wealthiest person on the planet?

- I do not feel that I am enough when I see other people's lives are just so perfect, and I cannot hide my feeling as I think that others' grasses are greener. Oh, especially when I hear people say something that reflects how good they are, I feel it demonstrates my lack. I cannot even take any more advice or suggestions because I feel these are all attacking and shaking my confidence.
- I feel guilty and ashamed when I make mistakes or lose a game. I am a failure.
- And the list goes on and on.

Dr. Con: "Look back at what you just said. It seems that you already know the answers to your problems. Let me explain to you."

- If you sleep better and find your passion, you should not feel tired.
- If you put all the time of your thoughts into immediate plans and actions, you shouldn't feel overwhelmed.
- If you lift your meaningless worries and anxiety and do not waste time being worried about something that hasn't happened, you will be fine. Why can't you look at what good things have already happened to you and count them? Count your blessings!
- If you always want to control others outside of you and change things outside of you, you will only be frustrated, disappointed, or upset. Because the only thing you can control is yourself. Don't expect others to go the same way as you do.
- If you want to achieve something, you must prepare with 'failures, pains, setbacks, efforts and more time.' Good things take time. If you are impatient, you will only give up easily and feel unfulfilled. Remember to chase progress, not perfection.

- If you are only wise and intelligent enough to realize that what you do isn't who you are, then you will understand that measuring your success isn't about what you do but how complete you can feel.

Then Dr. Con will ask: "Did you ever try to do something to let go of these problems?"

Mr. Subcon: "Of course I do. I do self-care, go shopping, eat what I love, do my nails, and dress up nicely some days; I even exercise. But you know, I do not feel like doing any of these some days. I am too tired to think, so my self-care is to do nothing"

Dr. Con: "But what you are saying is like when you bump your head, you put a bandage? When you are bleeding, will you take some medicine instead of doing first-aid to stop the bleeding?"

Most Mr. Subcons will say: "Well, whatever, I am just going to keep moving on, and it will be a new day tomorrow." He hides his problem, ignores it, and makes excuses to move on, but a few days later, Mr. Subcon faces all the above challenges again because he never really 'let it go.'

To be an excellent self-management doctor of your emotion and soul, you must have this attitude. It would help if you said to yourself: "Ok, there were the pains I had before, and even those I had yesterday and last minute. I am not feeling complete, and I need help, and I am willing to do what you say to let it go because if I don't, the ultimate victim will be myself."

It would help if you confessed to yourself, too, because the moment you decide to face it, Dr. Con starts his magic. He tells Subcon who the boss is. You control your minds. If you decide to let Mr. Subcon lead your mind, Dr. Con will keep reminding you and making noises where you will never find real peace. Both are in you. You cannot ignore your Mr. Subcon because it results from your past experiences and habits if you don't let them have a deep conversation. **If you instead go outside yourself to find solutions, the spiritual illness will never be healed.**

In other words, many people may find something unrelated to feeling better. Someone smokes, someone takes drugs, someone drinks alcohol, or plays games, whatever it is, the thing that makes you addicted but never really helps you to sort out your problem. It will only create more new problems.

My bad habit of making myself feel better was 'shopping,' I could buy things I didn't need when I was much younger because I thought that would be the only time I could rest and do whatever I wanted. Later, I found it was time-wasting and money-consuming too. Not highly recommended.

I do cleaning and sorted out my wardrobe or tidied up the room if I worked too much or was stressed. It was helpful to distract me from these things for a while, but it never really helped to sort out the root problem. However, besides making my home a better place, it does also help a lot for my mental health. Here is a beneficial article that can help you to do a yearly cleaning checklist:

Simple Yearly Cleaning Checklist | Free Printable Download (moritzfinedesigns.com)

Link:https://www.moritzfinedesigns.com/yearly-cleaning-checklist/

What are the fundamental ways you should do to let it go? Will you create more problems to hide from the old issues, or will you face them and admit them so you can deal with them? Will you go with your old patterns but expect a breakthrough? If your old routine didn't help you to change, how could it transform you magically and suddenly? No way.

The life-changing 'let it go' moment started with 'confession or surrender.' If you are not confessed or surrender your true feelings, you will never find the moment of 'letting go.'

How to be burden-free from self-healing?
I have concluded these **six simple steps** to let go genuinely, but you must promise to take them into practice and action. Even if you take baby steps, promise me you will never stop trying. However, *Roman isn't built in one day*. Getting started and keep trying is the key. To highlight: if you are in an impaired physical and mental health position, please always seek the doctor and specialist's advice. These self-healing processes wouldn't help you to sort out the whole problem.

However, to live a better life to let it go, here are the guiding steps for you:
Step one: Doctor Appointment / You must find time to do it.

If you don't make time for Mr. Sub-Con to meet Dr. Con of you, you won't have time for the next steps. It is all about priority. **Make a doctor's appointment** yourself, and you must find the time. It is your priority. If you don't settle yourself, and if you don't take care of yourself, you can't take care of anybody else. You, as Dr. Con, must put your patient first. It is all about priorities.

What I mean by that is you also need to set up a schedule to **spend time with** yourself and **for** yourself. Yes, you must put it into your agenda, or everything else will easily take your time as priorities. Find a safe and relaxing room where you can have a clear mind. Do you hear that so many people are doing meditations nowadays? Give yourself a short time to breathe to clear your mind. I suggest you do it in the very early morning. Especially when everybody else is still sleeping and quiet, nothing could bother you or stress you out.

To do this, you need only one commitment to yourself and allow yourself to have that personal space, between 15 minutes to an hour. Please don't stress out if others say you must do it in 30 minutes or an hour. Everybody's schedule is different, and everybody's life is different. For some of you who are parents, maybe your kids will call you anytime, so 15 minutes is a great start. If you can insist on doing it every day, you will see a magical transformation in your life in how much more you understand about yourself and your soul.

And please promise me, put your mobile phone away or anything that could distract you away. Just focus on searching for yourself by spending time with yourself and listening to yourself. *If you are a believer, spending spiritual time with God will be better because it's better that your mind* **is filled with God's grace and words than nothing.** Someone likes to follow YouTube Meditation. Anything that helps you truly make time for yourself. The simplest thing is to sit in a quiet place earlier in the morning without interruption and focus on breathing.

One of the most important things you must be aware of is mobile phone time. If you search online about Mobile phones' negative impact, there will be various research to show you.

Suggest you check out these to raise your awareness and help you to transform your bad habits:

40 Harmful Effects Of Mobile Phones On Brain, Eyes, And Health (latikaeyeandmaternityclinic.com)
    Link: https://www.latikaeyeandmaternityclinic.com/harmful-effects-of-mobile-phones/
    7 Negative Effects of Mobile Phones on Society – Addiction Tips
    Link: https://www.addictiontips.net/phone-addiction/negative-effects-of-mobile-phones-on-society/

Let me ask: **"Is your mobile phone more important than your health?"** If your answer is no, you must make time for your health—particularly your spiritual and mental health in this perspective. Then make time for yourself.

- *Step two: Diagnose / To seek, and you will find.*

Use your **Dr. Con to meet Mr. Subcon** to **seek and find** your issue— That's when people are meditating to dig out their inner feelings, solve the problem, and align their minds to the right way. Except for meditation, you must write them down in a journal.

No matter whether you are doing meditation or writing. You need to **dig o**ut the inner fear and pain of your past to let it go. It must be through a conversation to find out the answers. What I mean by that is you must ask good questions to find out where you are and how you can help yourself to heal your broken heart or anything hidden in your heart for a long time.

Write down your pain and struggles and **find** the cause if you can. It may be lots of pain points and lots of possible causes. Write them all down so you can be aware of your confirmed diagnosis. Sometimes you may need time to find out why by seeing others' life to reflect on you. Find out anything that you care about, no matter if it is negative emotions or not. Every emotion is a sign of something that hides deep in your heart.

You are not going to find out all answers all at once or within one time or one week. It is like a friendship. The more you spend time with your friends, the more you learn about them.

- *Step three: To admit, confess and surrender.*

Admit, confess, and surrender that you are not in control of things out of your hands that are outside of you; the only thing you can control is everything inside of you.

What I mean by that is most of the time, we want to take control of everything we can. When we love, we want to control our kids to do what we want them to do. When we are hurt, we want to hold ourselves and do many things to avoid being hurt again. We want to avoid trying when rejected because we just want to feel good.

My previous conversations with myself are always like: Yes, I am ok, I will be ok, and I will get there, which is very good for self-encouragement, but it is not helpful to find my struggles or understand more about myself. It takes me so long to realize that admitting, confessing, and surrendering is one of the bravest things and the best things to honor myself and my feeling. Because if I don't, all I am trying to do is to avoid the problem, and when I don't deal with the problem, the problem will always come back to deal with me.

I always thought to confess that I was feeling down or sad made me look bad and weak, but I was wrong. Our conversation can be like, Ok, I am not feeling ok, and I don't know why, but I know I will be ok once I change my perspective, and I want to know why I am not feeling ok. Then it will start to dig out more and more of your true feelings from you. Remember, never judge yourself for your emotions because everyone else could have the same feelings, and they must be caused by something. ***That is the most significant step before your transformation if you can confess (admit/acknowledge).***

Write them down why you are not ok, then also write down why you should let it go. The more answers you can list, the better. Such as letting it go will make you more joyful. To make you healthy and to allow more space for better things. Or what happened before already happened that there's nothing you could change, so you must look at the future. Also, an essential part that you must remember is that your past does not define you. Your choice of whom you want to become in the future determines you. Every day is a new day for you to press a restart button. Every fresh breath of yours is a unique chance for you to press a restart button because none of us is still living in the past, we are all here now, and we will be somewhere in the future!

- *Step four: Find the medicine / To affirm and declare.*

Affirm and declare that you are the only one in control and can take control of your mind and your choices. **You are the leader of your life.** Write your affirmation down and declare. There will be a separate page regarding the affirmation words you can use.

- *Step Five: Take the medicine / To start letting go.*

Read your affirmations and remind yourself daily is your medicine. Indeed start to let go of anything that doesn't belong to you. Drive your mind to a beautiful place wherever makes you feel peaceful and happy.

Everything takes time, but everything starts with a small step which is the giant step to commerce.

I remember that when I was so down and doubting myself. Every time I read inspirational words and start declaring about them and affirming them, I feel better immediately.

- *Step Six: Take it regularly until it's healed / To practice and repeat.*

Practice makes perfect, and repetition is the magic to build up muscle for you.

Every morning, check things you have that make you grateful, write at least one thing each morning, and read them the following day but still remind yourself one sentence: **nothing of these will be forever, so live in and embrace this feeling and cherish this moment.**

Every night, before sleep, tell yourself that you decide to let go of anything that doesn't serve you and forgive anybody that potentially hurt you or offended you, including yourself. Forgive anything you do wrongly, and ultimately let it go. *Tell yourself to let it go is the only way for you to break the chain of the past and live the best of your own life.*

Do all these things daily and **remember that these are part of our successful and enjoyable journey.** *If you don't take the lead, your emotion will lead you.*

The most important thing you need to understand is: To hate

someone can last forever, and it will never go away; To forgive someone will only take a bit of time, and it will go away forever. We must shake off all heavy burdens with all the old shadows to have a fresh new mind, body, and spirit for our future.

Great, now we have known who we are, how to love ourselves and others, how to count our blessings and let go of the burden that we can live at present, but how about our future? What if when we face big fears in life? Worries about our future. What can we do?

CHAPTER FIVE

Joyful leading Faith.

Lead to Turn off your false alarm mechanisms.

I choose to know myself deeper, stay awake, take my faith, and turn off my false alarm mechanism.

Do you always feel angry, worried, and fearful? When there was some exciting thought coming into your mind, then instead of transferring it to a good outcome, you hesitated, over-thought, then it became frustrations, anger, or worries hanging in your mind. Everyone would have faced these moments, and I conclude it to be the bad guy's fear. Fear will cause anger, stress, worries, and more.

I live in one of the best living cities and the most extended lockdown city Melbourne, Australia. Because of the COVID lockdown, many fears are coming out from there. People are suffering from different types of worries.

One of my friends, to keep it private, I will call her Cecelia. Cecelia has a daughter with health issues. According to the doctor, who said that if her daughter had got COVID, she would be too weak to handle the illness, and you could imagine how much stress and fear she had to carry... ... So, when COVID hit, she was distraught and decided to stay home more than go out. Because whenever she wanted to go out, she would think that it could potentially bring her daughter a higher risk of death. But then the other problem came up.

Because they had been staying home for so long that fear she was holding, she would have gone anywhere by using sanitizer all day and so many sanitary processes. That made her exhausted not just physically but also mentally. She almost found herself depressed because of all these. Then the psychologist saw her and said something like an awakening call.

Here is what the psychologist roughly said: Fear is apparent, and when your body is facing a high risk of a safety threat, you should be fearful because that helps to avoid some potential attack. For example, if someone holds a gun and points it at you. Anything outside that is called stress.

After hearing that, my acquaintances were that because of being afraid of the 'potential' risk that can bring to you, you stopped functioning entirely. That's anxiety, not fear. Fear can be healthy, but stress can be very unhealthy and can potentially cause many problems.

So, I told my friend: "You know, it is like if we are afraid that someone will throw some vases from the high buildings or something from tall buildings potentially fall anytime. Does it mean we should NEVER STEP OUT of OUR HOUSE? To avoid that 'Potential Risk'?

If that's the way you live, stay away from any potential risks, the fear will ruin your life and prevent good things from happening in your future.

Once my friend was aware of that, she started to step out of her 'false alarm fear' zone, and their life started to go back to normal, and they became much more joyful again.

Like many of you, I am facing the same issue, and we are unaware of many potential challenges. For example, I have always been very good at meeting people and being social. Still, I found it tough to go shopping or talk to someone because it needs lots of practice about what to say and how to say things correctly so I won't hurt people's feelings. I found the more I thought, the more fearful I became.

Be alerted of the false alarm fear in your life, and remember to turn it off, but how to conquer fear and train your anti-fear muscles?

Fear's Enemy- Faith. Believing in yourself and others.

Faith is to believe before we see. If we can see, it is not faith; it is simply a sight. One of the most powerful things you can do is to believe in others before they even believe in themselves.

There's an important thing we must acknowledge, which is that 'Faith' and 'Fear' won't exist simultaneously. In other words, we shouldn't be fearful if we are faithful enough. Being authentic and frightening don't exist at the same time. When you are afraid, which means you are not feeling trustworthy enough, you are worried about something. When you are faithful enough, no fear could find a way to go in and attack you.

In my dictionary, except for love, there isn't a more powerful word you can find than 'to believe, ' which relies on your faith. From where does your confidence come?

We have a tough choice every day that we must make. We need to choose either faith' or 'fear.' Faith and fear have something in common. Except for both words starting with F, they are all related to 'the unseen.' When we have faith, we can't see it, but we have a vision and believe that something good will happen. While we are afraid, we can't see it, but we have worries and believe that something terrible will happen.

Many people will judge each other that they are brainwashed by something. They will laugh at each other for their choice of putting the wrong information and thoughts into their mind. Let's be honest:

Aren't we brainwashed every day? But we get to choose what water we will use to wash our brains. If we don't choose wisely the water we use to clean, it will likely be dirty, making our brains more confused and sadder. If you believe in the unknown is 'fear,' then your life will be full of 'fear,' and if you believe in the mystery is 'faith' instead, then your life will be full of peace and joy because faith produces good fruits. If you still think 'fear' is what you choose and what you want, then 'faith' will not be able to have its place in you.

Why do positive people become more positive and negative people become more damaging if they don't change what information they choose to listen to and what they choose to believe? If they decide to stay where they are and are unwilling to accept new things or be open to new messages, they will never know if it's good or bad.

It makes a huge difference when you know where to put your faith. Where do you put your trust? How important is it to have 'faith.'? Because to do everything starts with 'faith.' Except for training our anti-fear muscles, training our' faith muscles' is critical. Because only if we have faith can we turn down any doubts or setbacks. How could we get there?

First, how powerful when you hear words like: I believe in you!

Why do others believe in you? Why do you believe in others?

I believe in everyone because I know we are the same human beings, and I know that as long as there's a will, there will be a way. Why do all those successful people or other inspirational speakers, including myself, keep saying to everyone that 'you can do it?' Because we all suffered doubts and tried before. I want you to know that if they could do it, and if anybody in the world could do it, you can do it too. There's only one thing that makes us different, which is our choices. People who believe, achieve, and disbelieve can't reach.

Why can't you keep believing if you know you can do it? Why can't you build up more self-confidence? Why do many of us lose our self-confidence and faith quickly? What do you believe? I have concluded two most important things to gain your deep faith besides your spiritual belief.

First, self-confidence
What is self-confidence? Self-confidence differs from trust and faith. Trust and loyalty are mutual, meaning we trust and have faith in somebody, not ourselves. Self-confidence is the inner confidence we find in ourselves; we do more things and achieve more to build it up.

You know the feeling when you do something successfully.

You know the feeling when you face obstacles and challenges but overcome them, and when you re-encounter them, you are confident to handle them.

You know the feeling when you know who you are and not be shrunk or doubted by others' comments.

But confidence is that even though you cannot achieve something at the moment, you believe you can achieve it someday or later. Or, even though you cannot do something, you know it doesn't change the fact that you can do what you do.

So many times, fear attacks me with words like "what if" and overwhelms me with stress in my daily work and life. If I don't handle it, it will attack my emotion and bring disaster to my relationships with anyone.

To conquer your fear and train your anti-fear muscle, you need to know the two main reasons. They are always related to two final things:

The first thing is the "fear of losing your self-esteem."
Defending our self-esteem is a common issue for almost everyone, especially younger generations. We are not saying Self-esteem isn't good, it is a great thing to have, but people miss the point of having it. If you google this word, it says the meaning of Self-esteem is confidence in one's worth or abilities and self-respect.

The misinterpretation in our life, how people see it, seems to be: Self-esteem is putting self-confidence in others' eyes, **winning others' agreement all the time, no failure is allowed, and respecting others' opinions about ourselves.**

Self-esteem is a superpower if we can understand its meaning and start to build it up by genuinely understanding it.

First, we must know that worries and the wrong way of fighting self-esteem cause two big problems:

1. **Lack of confidence** (Afraid of failure or trying new things.)

Fearing failure is one of the most common problems everyone could have. Most of the time, we want to look good and do something we know will show us how capable we are.

The fact is that the less we try new things, the less confident we will become. Our muscles of confidence will become weaker if we don't practice it.

My older daughter is fantastic at many things, but her biggest challenge is being afraid of losing or failing. One day she could be thrilled and confident when she won a race or competition, but another day she could be super upset and unconfident when she just lost a small game. No matter how many times we tried to tell her it was ok, we were supposed to enjoy the process more, not just the outcome, which still did not help to change the situation immediately.

I realized it is her worries and anxiety, the thoughts of self-esteem, that are telling her that to lose means she is not good enough. It shakes her self-identity. It brings her a lack of confidence each time she loses a game. She will feel like being the end of the world.

She is also very cautious about trying new things; she'd love to stay in her safe zone to make herself look better. She worries that if things go wrong, she will lose her self-esteem. We had to take her trying more things, and she made it every time after trying one newer something.

Her confidence came back more. We will share how to be confident and remain confident later.

2. Lack of growth and breakthrough (We discussed this in the previous chapters. However, for this share, we highlighted that a person who isn't humble enough could not be teachable or learn more. Only remaining hungry can bring you transformational change.)

Many people continuously feel content with who they are and what they have nowadays. It might be good to remain grateful, but it may be harmful when you never raise your standard.

I only studied for a little while. I graduated when I was only 17-18 from Uni, and I skipped three years of high school and just attended 1-year preparation school before college. Was I too bright or intelligent? No, I had to graduate earlier because I saw my family struggle with money, and I had to be independent as soon as possible to support my parents.

I had always been hungry to learn and grow, even though I graduated and started to work earlier. I remember the first year I started working, I got paid, sent an incredible amount of money back to my parents, and told them I no longer needed their money, so it was time for me to pay them from then on. That was the first financial breakthrough in my life.

I also invested myself in night school and kept learning Piano and Spanish. I never want to stop learning and trying new things. I felt so good about my life.

However, after getting married, I enjoyed my status for a few years when I got enough monthly income. Most of the time, except for working, it seems what I could think of or discuss with families in HKG was where to eat excellent food and have fun. I had great fame in the company and ran a great team. That was one of the most extended times I felt for at least three to five years when I felt something important was missing. I got unhappy or grumpy quickly, and no matter how many materials I owned, I couldn't feel joyful.

Until one day, a deep inner voice reminded me that I would never stop learning or growing because I knew my value would only increase with my knowledge and experience growth. It turned out to be true! So, I decided to change! I changed how I enjoyed my comfortable zone, which was a dangerous place to be.

Looking back, all the best decisions I made that brought me break throughs were all those uncomfortable and hard decisions.

One of the most significant decisions was to quit one of the best jobs in HK with high pay coming to Australia to restart my life; The other decision was to resign from a high position in a substantial global organization to start my own business. Both decisions made me so uncomfortable, and they were scary. But they were so rewarding and were the best decisions I ever had. I never settled. I moved from one city to another to chase my dream and to break my comfort zone. But, whenever I found 'growth' and 'breakthrough,' I found joy!

Through seeing my kids going to school learning, seeing myself experiencing from company to company, and seeing people from various backgrounds, cultures, and industries. I found it fascinating that *our life is a school where we will only graduate once we close our eyes and stop breathing. Going to school isn't just about learning knowledge but also about bringing good and bad things to our life experiences. We may graduate from one school and then the next to equip us with stronger minds to face new challenges. But our life will keep going, so if we think we graduate, then we can use the knowledge to meet everything in life, that's not true. Life is far more complicated than just using your knowledge. Life needs your continuous attention. Only if you are willing to grow more to serve your life will it grow and help you back!*

So many successful people withdrew from school very early for multiple reasons, but they turned out to be the most successful or happiest person. Why? Because they were hungry and remain hungry, hunger is your best gift. I am not encouraging you to withdraw from your school or stop learning from school. But I want you to understand that the key is not about going to school; it is about your hunger to learn no matter where you are.

Check out this article:
Link: https://people.howstuffworks.com/15-notable-people-who-dropped-out-of-school.htm
20 Notable People Who Dropped Out of School | HowStuffWorks
By: the Editors of Publications International, Ltd. & Melanie Radzicki McManus | Updated: Aug 2, 2022

The 20 notable people mentioned in this article are **Thomas Edison, Benjamin Franklin, Albert Einstein, John D. Rockefeller, Walt Disney, Princess Diana, George Burns, Colonel Sanders, Charles Dickens, Elton John, Ray Kroc, Harry Houdini, Whoopi Goldberg, Ringo Starr, Richard Branson, Jennifer Lawrence, Sachiin Tendulkar, Mary Pickford, and Julie Andrews.**

It says: "Singer Robyn Rihanna Fenty is the best-selling digital artist in the world, as well as being an entrepreneur, fashion designer, and actor — accomplishments all achieved sans a high school diploma. Rihanna was born in 1988 in Barbados. In 2003, she was discovered by two New York City music producers vacationing in the Caribbean. The 15-year-old quit high school and moved to the Big Apple, where the record label Def Jam released her debut album. Today, Rihanna has sold more than 54 million albums and 210 million tracks and is the youngest solo artist to have 14 No. 1 singles on the Billboard Hot 100. She's also designed collections for Armani and has hugely successful fashion and beauty lines."

"In 1918, while still in high school, future Oscar-winning film producer and theme park pioneer Walt Disney began taking night courses at the Academy of Fine Arts in Chicago. Disney dropped out of high school at age 16 to join the Army, but because he was too young to enlist, he joined the Red Cross with a forged birth certificate instead. Disney was sent to France, where he drove an ambulance covered from top to bottom with cartoons that eventually became his film characters. After becoming the multimillionaire founder of the Walt Disney Company and winning the Presidential Medal of Freedom, Disney received an honorary high school diploma at age 58."

So many people learned a lot and were the best students at school but ended up not fulfilling much in their life. Why? Because they thought they were good enough with their knowledge and there was no need to keep learning more. Or they are too afraid of making mistakes. What I found is that most top students are always perfectionists. However, by saying that, good students can also be very successful if they know what they want and never stop learning. Their primary knowledge is already good, so it is easier for them to learn things, which is why we need to be careful that we, humans, hate but love to be challenged simultaneously. We hate because our flesh hates pain, but we love every time after pain; when we gain, the joy comes through.

Without a breakthrough, it will cause one alternative pain: a lack of fulfillment. Because achieving fulfillment only comes from making efforts. **In other words, we need to do hard things to have more joy in life.** We will find more joy in self-growth.

Until one day, I realized the **secret weapon** to conquer the fear of 'losing self-esteem.'

The first story I want to share is about learning to speak a new language.

I could speak English, Mandarin, and Cantonese, and I could talk about a bit of Spanish, Japanese, and some local native languages in mainland China, where I was born and where I ever heard more often.

You may say: Wow, you are so talented in learning a new language, but listen, I believe everybody could be qualified to learn how to do anything if they know the secret weapon because I have so many friends from everywhere in the world that some of them even could speak more than 16 languages. Is it because they are genius? Is it because I am more intelligent than you? No, I'm afraid I have to disagree, and I don't think so.

English isn't my first language, but I loved it so much, and from the first day I learned it, I couldn't stop learning. I loved learning it to find any chance to speak and practice. It was tough when you started learning a new language. The hardest part isn't that you don't know how to learn to talk, it is the part that you are not afraid of trying, and you let go of your eagle and unnecessary self-esteem and pride. Why do I say it?

When I learned English, I couldn't speak properly, and when I faced things I didn't know, I still dared to say them wrongly so that people would point them out, and then the next moment, I could speak them accurately. When I first spoke Cantonese, there was so much teasing moment by those native speakers when I mispronounced some words. But I found it a joy to me, and I enjoyed speaking even if it was wrong because I would either say it correctly or make people laugh badly to bring them joy. How good is that? That attitude helped me so much in learning any new language. As long as I wasn't afraid of making mistakes, I could only speak better and better.

Remember when babies learn to speak? They have so many words spoken inaccurately, but what will they do? Never speak again? No, they will keep talking until they can express it rightly. Why are kids better learners than us? Except for the point that scientists said that kids' brains from a certain age would be the quickest time for learning because they had more time to play, sleep, and focus with fewer distractions. I always believe that one of the biggest things is that they are young and are not afraid to try again. They have less fear. Much fewer doubts or hesitation than adults. Because as adults, as we grow up, the older we become, the more judgment we hear, and the more we always want to look good and feel good. The less humble we become and less teachable we become as well.

So, the first thing of a secret weapon is to be 'humble and teachable.'

I want to share one of the common challenges everybody could face. We all know stage fear is one of the biggest fears that almost everyone faces. I have always dreamed of being a speaker, a singer, or a dancer on stage. When I got many opportunities to participate in Karaoke gatherings or singing competitions, and after a few setbacks in my mind that I was worried about losing my self-esteem, I was hungrier to try to experience it. So, I said yes to almost every show and opportunity to be on the stage.

I remember I started from being afraid and shy to being calm and enjoyable. Thus, the secret weapon is **"Don't overthink. Just do it! Practice makes perfect!"** There is a reason behind the slogan of the Nike brand. "Just Do It!" We all need this reminder daily!

Being humble and teachable instead of fearing losing self-esteem helped me achieve what I have and who I am today. I attended almost all activities I could participate in at school and college. Participation in stage performances or basketball games taught me many life experiences and emotions I could have never experienced if I had only looked and observed. I loved that adventure of conquering fear, and I became better and better each time. I am so grateful that I chose to be proactive and to try! It helped me build up many good things and a courageous spirit.

Another story is about when I was first assigned to travel overseas. I remember it was Vietnam, and I needed to go alone. I was only 19, not even 20. I was so excited and nervous at the same time. I knew I could not say no because this was the dream career I wanted. To travel around the world and learn more about people. But back then, I heard so many bad stories about how unsafe Vietnam is, especially as a young female my age if I travelled alone. There were so many negative thoughts and messages attacking me.

I had a choice in front of me, to say no and stay where I was, and do what I did. Or I could choose to be the courageous one, take a great adventure and experience if it is what the others were saying about Vietnam. I decided to go!! It was one of the best experiences ever!

It gave me so much more confidence to travel alone anywhere in the world without fear, and people there welcomed me so well, and I could have my own story to tell people rather than what others were saying.

People who never visited China and only heard of stories there still put it as an image of 50 years ago, and some were afraid to go. Instead, those who ever visited have been visiting and loved to be there. Many foreigners moved to Shanghai, and it is one of the best cities in the world. Let alone all political issues in every country. My point here is to try before you conclude. **People's experiences can be different from yours.**

It is essential to learn **anti-fear awareness and skills**. Always think and ask yourself, and if you find it is a false alarm fear, embrace the challenge, and the more you try, the less anxiety will leave in you. You will be surprised that you could become one of the most fearless people on the planet. It doesn't mean you can face all dangerous situations; it just brings you more courage and strength to handle more uncertainties.

How do you be confident and remain confident? People always ask me, how could you be so confident all the time? I finally concluded the 7Ps so that they can also benefit you.

7 Ps

Process your past.
Proactively and practically learn and develop high-value skills.

Problems bring opportunity.
Prevent being arrogant.
Practice makes perfect.
Progress, not perfection.
Power of 'I believe in you.'

1. Process your past.
We had one chapter that mentioned letting go. Diving in the past is a waste of time. However, it is crucial to process our history to dig out the garbage in us before we put nice and new things in, which applies seriously to your self-confidence built up work too.

Search or check studies about how childhood life impacts our adulthood. Without a doubt, it has a massive impact on the true stories of myself and the people around me. If we ignore it, avoid it, hide it, and don't want to talk about it. The potential wounds can come out and badly affect your adult life and damage your self-confidence. Then it potentially destroys your new life, which you live now, not in the past.

To be confident, I think it is super important to find your scars from childhood or your past and take some time to process them and let them go.

It is interesting that if we have a physical scar, it won't hurt if we press it, but if it is an emotional or spiritual scar, it can hurt a lot if we don't know how to process it and let it go.

The best way to let it go is to face it, embrace it, and use it.

I felt very unconfident for a long time when I was little, as people always compared me with my older sister, who is only one year older than me. Words like: Your sister is prettier than you. You look older than she. She is slim, and you are fat.

It brought me so many scars and made me so unconfident, and I started believing she was better. That's when I began searching for my inner beauty because I thought she was better looking than me, but I could find something better than looking. Because of that, I did so much to build my inner confidence and make efforts to be the one who thinks more for others and always lets others feel good spending time with me.

See, I found out my scar caused my weakness. I faced it, embraced it, and then used it to transform myself into a better version. Then whenever people repeat the same thing, I would say yes, but I am beautiful in different ways. I also realized that everyone has different tastes, so when someone says that I am not the type they think is as beautiful, it doesn't change the fact that I am beautiful on my way. See, when there's a carrot, a person who hates it will say it's disgusting, but someone who loves it will say it is so yummy. The carrot doesn't change its value, and it is still a healthy vegetable with vitamin B. You need to know your self-worth.

I didn't have many new clothes to wear when I was little, and I always had to wear second-hand ones or sometimes very old-fashioned clothes, so I became very obsessed with fashion afterward when I could earn and buy my clothes. If I use it as a gift, it will be a great skill, but if I overuse it, like buying too much, it can cause a need for more confidence.

Then I started to face my scar, embraced my weakness again, and chose to work out more rather than buy fashionable things. I feel more confident when I am doing work-out regularly, and I look much better with a better body shape. Besides, the weakness brought me good outcomes in selecting fashion and increasing my good taste in style too. Now I got a win-win outcome. Happy about processing my fault into strengths and gaining one more skill.

The day when you are open to talking about the old pain and scars is the day you process it to another level. Because you could then find a chance to let go and re-navigate it to your life with a positive impact.

What did your Lack in your childhood? What are the things that you used to lack but do not anymore? Would you do me a favor? Find them, don't avoid them.

Find them, face them, embrace these pains and scars, and use them. Every pain we have is supposed to be helpful to transform us to be better. It is to share with others and help others, or it is to define you to be more confident and use them to become more powerful than ever.

2. Proactively and practically learn and develop high-value skills. We talked about how we become more valuable in the 'false alarm' chapter. To be confident, we must learn new skills and proactively develop high-value skills.

You may feel stressed if this means you will have to do many things to learn and grow. No, you don't, because you already have it.

Everybody has a special gift, which doesn't have to be huge. Sometimes a tiny soft skill is much more powerful than anything.

Can you list something you are good at from these lists?

Singing, Dancing, Arts, Communication, Speaking, Listening, Sports, Fashion, Caring, Loving, Marketing, Hosting, Learning, or any skills which won't be out of date?

Why is it so important?

Because if we are good at something specific, it helps us to strengthen our confidence.

Why am I confident even though I am not good at many other things? For example, I am good at leadership, my work, and so on, but I need to improve at something that requires me to read long instruction books. I'd instead find someone to ask or to help. In any circumstance, my husband is good at what I am not good at, but it doesn't change my confidence. Why? Because I am good at communicating, learning, and what I love and am passionate about doing.

We don't have to be the same, and we don't have to know everything. We need to have common sense, but we don't have to know everything to be confident. If you are willing to learn and develop high-valued skills proactively, I mean intentionally, which will help to lift your confidence every time.

The task for you. Find something you are passionate about, which you used to be good at and capable of. In other words, one of your habits. Do it today, and it will bring your confidence to another level.

Is it ice skating, surfing, hiking, basketball, football, photography, painting, drawing, singing, or dancing? Build up your bucket list and start to do them.

3. Problem brings opportunity.

Sometimes a big problem can shake our self-confidence if we don't like to see or deal with it.

"Wait, what? Problem? I don't like any problems." you may say. Why do we need to have problems? First, nobody loves dealing with issues, but it is essential to understand that to build our confidence, we realize that we have daily problems to solve. If we don't deal with them, the Problem will deal with us. To be more confident, you must understand that problems will bring us more opportunities.

Did you ever solve a problem before? How did you feel back? How did you feel afterward? Wasn't it evident once you resolved the issue, your self-confidence level upgraded straight away?

But what if you didn't end up solving the Problem? But how about the process? How about soft skills? Did you use your talents? Communication, listening, or caring? Wasn't that an excellent opportunity for you to shine if you got these skills?

4. Prevent being arrogant.

We tend to be confused about whether feeling confident is being arrogant or the other way around.

Below is how I see the difference:

Being confident means knowing you are good; you can do anything! You can handle any challenges! It is not relying on comparing to anybody else. You still appreciate people, and you can still be humble and teachable. The confident language will say, "I believe I can do it!" "I am good." "I am excellent."

When we say being arrogant means exaggerating your confidence and showing that you are better than anybody else. Whatever you do, you consistently compare with others, feel you are better than others, and ignore other people's strengths or potential talents. You don't want to see it because you believe you are better. You have no room to learn, and all you are thinking about is self-centered. The arrogant language will say, "I believe I can do better than you or anybody else." "I am better than anybody, and I am the best." "I am so good and will never let others be better than me." "I am more special and precious than others."

It is essential to be confident, but very dangerous to be arrogant. It can ruin your future.

Being confident can still keep you growing and learning from others. Your confidence will only grow more because it helps you to grow and learn faster! It can also empower people that people could see your light and want to be close to you. You will have more and more friends, and you will be successful in life and work.

While being arrogant can only create your little world with satisfaction, you no longer have a humble heart to keep learning and growing. You cannot see people around you, and you won't be grateful because you think you are the only one who is smart enough to contribute; others are lower than you. The outcome of arrogance is that you will be blind to the truth and joy! You will only be self-centered and lonely. You will be angry easily because you cannot put down your pride, you cannot hide your eagle, and your eagle scared people away from you.

I will be alright if I don't have some friends or only a few friends. But you know what? People won't care for you back if you don't care about people. The best way to receive is to give first.

So always be the leader to self-check if there are many choices you made because you think you are better or you can do it even though you know others can do it too; you choose to focus on competing yourself, not comparing or competing with others.

Change your leadership language to "I can do anything, and I can be the best version of myself. I love to appreciate others, and I don't compare with anybody because I know we have something different to learn from each other."

5. Practice makes perfect

There's magic in Practice.

Being a leader is also a process of learning and being a student simultaneously. Every leader is also a great student of education. A great teacher is also a great learner. If you stop learning, you cannot keep being a great teacher.

Remind yourself of all your goodness and constantly remind the previous success you have achieved so far. Not to boast your pride but to boast your confidence.

When we face challenges, it's so easy to get discouraged or scared. Here are three things you can do.

One, count your success.

Grab a paper and write down as many things you have done well. You can have a super long list, and you can read that list at least once a day or a week. Whenever you look at that list, you will realize how many great things you achieved and how much more you can achieve.

Two, do a daily hard thing challenge.

Do a new hard thing every day. For instance, to have a conversation with a stranger or to challenge your comfort zone. These habits can create so much more confidence in you every time. Despite the result, it helps you become more confident whenever you try new things.

Three, do daily self-encouraging words and gestures.

Two things are magical and beneficial if you do it daily, especially in the morning when you wake up and at night before sleep.

The first thing is to say powerful words and do self-affirmation.

Look at yourself in the mirror, say good words, and do it for 3 minutes or longer if you want. Words like: I am good, I am blessed, I am beautiful, I am unique, I am powerful, and I can do anything. Try it, and it brings you so much magic. Remember to smile when you do it. I had one coaching section with 30 people, they all tried, and they immediately felt the difference only for that 1-minute trial. Why don't you do it every day?

The second thing is to do powerful and energetic activities.

Daily 3 minutes will improve your confidence and performance. I usually will do or encourage my family with a model catwalk at home for fun, but seriously too. Even if it's 1 minute, it helps me to be more openly confident and accept and love myself more. There's also a reason why dancing creates confidence. Any activity that suits you. High-five yourself in the mirror is another good one, which allows you to improve your self-confidence. Besides, I remember when I was little that I played so many games pretending to be the role I wanted to become. The more I acted and pretended, the more I became like that person. So, your choice, catwalk, dance, high-five yourself in the mirror, or do a future target role play all work to help you improve your self-confidence.

6. *Process, not perfection*

Transformation takes time! The Process is not perfection!

You must focus on the Process, not the outcome or perfection, which is why to be confident adequately that you must show compassion to yourself and the people around you.

To be confident doesn't mean that you need to know everything. It means that despite knowing things you don't know, you can still be confident to have a conversation and connection with people. Most of the time, we always think a person needs to be the best to be confident in doing things, and that's not the case.

A person who may not be good at everything his friends can do can be more confident in who he is and what he can do. The same thing you can see is that so many experts are good at what they are doing that they may not be confident enough to speak in front of people.

To be confident, we must embrace the Process, not the perfection. We must show compassion for ourselves and allow ourselves to learn from every experience. Encourage us to get involved in more conversations by asking 'silly or stupid questions. There were many times when we were in a big event when most people didn't know what the speaker was talking about, but only a few people were willing to raise questions. They might look bad, but in the deep hearts of the majority, they show high respect for his honesty. That is called confidence.

Confidence isn't to avoid making mistakes. It is to be fearless, take responsibility for any decision you make, and not afraid to make new mistakes and learn.

7. *Power of 'I believe in you.'*
Finally, but not least, the power of 'I believe in you.'

Most of us know how powerful it is when we believe in ourselves, which is why so many of us seek more self-confidence because we know if we find it, we will do everything better and with the best outcomes.

However, I want to share something different. Because the fascinating truth I found is that sometimes a person says: I believe in you, is more potent than you say it yourself. We cannot deny that.

So, what I want you to know and use is to believe in yourself and others.

If you believe in others, you will see a magical turn-point in your life. If you start to think and encourage others more, you will receive much more than your self-centered efforts. Try to say 'I believe in you' in every person and everyday life, even though that person is imperfect and can be mean. Why? Here are two reasons.

One, the only time we do something terrible to others is because we also lack in that area, which means if we try to fill that gap with positive words to that person, it helps them to become a better version of themselves.

Two, the power of I believe in you to strangers or people you don't know can be a life-saving and life-changing moment for a person. Most of the time, a person who hears someone, even though it is from a stranger, who says good things about them, would believe it and remember it forever if that's something they need to hear. It costs nothing to say, 'I believe in you in someone's life today.

I wish I could count how many success stories I had with people around me who became much better versions of themselves; because of that, I said: 'I believe in you ". I showed them what I thought of them.

I believed them before they even believed themselves.

Many times, someone was mean to me and nasty to me. I chose to calm down and respond with something better to encourage them to reflect on their better side. I saw their behaviours dramatically switch to a better track as time passed. The reason is simple. We all have a better version of ourselves. Our better performance will permanently hide unless they find someone who believes in them. It's always more effective to help others dig into the better version than digging your own. That is why we all need help to dig into each other's better versions, and one of the valuable ways is to say words: "I believe in you!"

There were so many days when I went out and started to search for people who were down and upset to give them a small encouragement, a nice word to cheer them up! You could tell that their rainy and cloudy mood became sunny straight away.

There was a video online from a Japanese school. The teacher always 'high-five' the kids every day before entering the classroom. That small action shows the student that she believes in them and alternatively says, 'I like you, and 'you are amazing!' You can tell the students are so much happier, and the outcome of their study became ten times more effective because of their increasing self-confidence.

There were many real-life stories that miracles happened simply because they didn't give up their HOPE. 'HOPE' is powerful. It gives us more faith to believe that 'Tomorrow is always a better day.'

False Alarm Enemy # TWO: Worries about tomorrow and the future.

Did you ever feel stressed or angry, except for feeling not respected or worried about people's judgment? Are you constantly worried about your future? The future of your career, company, business, health, finance, relationship crisis, etc. Are you concerned about failure or looking bad when you say something wrong? Are you just anxious for nothing? We all have these moments. You are not alone. The problem is our minds, so let's explore more and fix our minds.

Worries about Money?

The most significant part of the false alarm comes from the worry of 'Money shortage,' which represents how much ability, capability, and flexibility I could have. So when I found out the root of the problem, it took me a long time to get into this and adjust myself. Trust me; once you dig into this, you will find a very fearless life!!!

One of the biggest worries to every one of us seems to be the 'Money Fear.' We always need to make sure that we have more money so that we do not need to worry about our life tomorrow or in the future. Without adjusting our money concept, the fear will never disappear.

First, money is a helpful tool, not evil itself, but we shouldn't love money. We should love the great things that we can achieve by using money. Without a good understanding of money, like all of you, I experienced an incredible sense of value before. One is that I love earning money and keep doing what I am doing to achieve more and more so that I can have more to do what I want to do. The other extreme point is I don't even want to earn much money, and all I was trying to do was to bring more kindness and build up a charity for everything I did. They both are not healthy.

We need to understand the good part if we manage money and let it serve us and the potentially lousy part if we 'love' money itself instead of 'loving what we could achieve as selfless purposes and goals' through cash. Most of you know what I meant. Once we know that we are the master of money, not the enslaved people, we shall be able to lead our life fearlessly instead of worrying about 'not having enough money.'

Do you think you are a rich person? Do you think you are poor because you have less money? Imagine one day you got lost on an island with no signal on your phone, and you still have your bank card and ID; what then? What do you need to find to make yourself happier to satisfy yourself? The famous Movie <<Cast Away >>teaches us when you are left on an island,

Why do people want to go on holiday on the island or far away from their homes? To see the beautiful views?

We purposely want to let a new environment remind us of the core things in life. It is not about how much money you earn, how beautiful you wear, or how famous or rich you are. It tells you that many things are more important than money and fame. These are the things that are essential to the concept built up in current society. But really? Nothing is more critical than a grateful heart! A healthy body! A moment you can still breathe!!!

Do you think money can buy happiness? You can buy a nice bed, but you cannot buy good sleep. You need to work on your mental health; You can buy excellent food, but you cannot buy a healthy body. You need to work on your physical health; You can buy a nice gift for yourself, but you cannot purchase others' love. It would be best if you worked on building relationships. There are more examples.

Money has many names:

- It can be called donations through charity.
- It's a fee when you need to pay for membership or school.
- It's called debt if you owe someone.
- It's called Tax when you pay the government.
- It's called fines if you pay the court.
- It can also be called salary, allowance, wages, loans, tips, or pension.
- If it's illegally receiving from someone with a political purpose, it is called a bribe.

You are wealthy not because you have the most money! You are rich not just because you have gained more life value but also because you are more potent and spiritually growing daily.

I was born in an impoverished city (materials-wise and economic-wise), with not much money in the family, and people just felt content if we could have food to eat and friends to play with, especially when I was little. My world was so simple. We were happy and felt rich! When I was little, sometimes, I had to make more friends so that when these naughty or bigger kids wanted to bully me or any younger ones, I could have someone more substantial standing by my side.

There weren't many toys invented then either, and money wasn't handy to us, mainly when we had little. We were very creative; we played games with no materials or stuff, set up rules, and as long as you got a team, games could get started, and it was so much fun! I realized then owning happiness was a choice, which was when I could find some friends to play with, then I was happy.

As time passed, I realized the pressure and burden on my family. Sometimes I could overhear my parents fighting because we did not have enough money to support the family, especially since I had a very hot-tempered dad. Because of money, I knew that some neighbours had to fight every day, and some sad stories might end up with couples who just got divorced. Very realistically sad.

The more I saw the burden on my parents' shoulders. The more determined that I would want to be independent and be able to support my family soon rather than being dependable. I chose to be hard-working, reminded myself to be humble, and kept learning. I found the best way to be unique and more valuable is to keep learning and growing daily. I loved singing, dancing, drawing, creativity, and anything related to art, and I always dreamed of becoming a successful artist. Nevertheless, I loved English as well. English was my second language, but from the first day I knew it, I fell in love with it and wanted to use it every day.

It was a solemn day when my mum asked me what subjects I preferred to learn on my next steps on a journey. It was precisely the roundabout of my life. I was struggling as I knew what I loved, but I knew what would be better for my family. Do you know the best part I learned about that day? My mum gave me the freedom to choose what I wanted to go next, which created love and an unselfish spirit around me. Because of her love and unselfishness, I started to think more about generosity. To be an artist is too expensive for my family, and I know to learn some skills like English trading, I could graduate earlier and start to support my family with my salary.

Even though I was only 14 years old, as long as I was willing to try, there was hope that I could release our family's financial burden. I chose to skip high school and give up my first loved dream to be an artist but go to a private Uni with 1-year prep-Uni, then I could study for three years Uni to finish my study. FYI, in China, private school was cheaper than public ones (the other way around compared to western countries unless it was an international school.)

So long story short, I did graduate from Uni when I was only 18. I started working when I was only 17 (as I was the youngest in the class and started much earlier than many other kids) while waiting for my graduation certificate and ceremony. I survived, and I worked harder than many other people. You see, it is never the age that stops you from achieving what you want. It may create some barriers, but you can avoid them.

Did you know I started my job when I arrived in Shenzhen on the third day from my hometown after the school holiday? I arrived on the first day and went to the 'Job Seeker Market' to interview companies randomly and see how it went. Trust me, I was so young, I didn't know what job I wanted to do, but there was one thing I learned. I wanted to be financially independent, and I wanted to try. So funny enough, I only needed to meet two companies, and they already said they would hire me.

I was an operational staff in the logistics industry and needed to learn what logistics meant when I had just started. I knew NOTHING about it, I got zero experience, waiting for my graduation certificate, but companies had already hired me. I started my job the very next day! To anyone struggling or worried about what if the position doesn't suit you. What if you didn't like it? What if they found I knew nothing about it? Would they fire me? Don't think about it too much. Try, and you will know. It's the same as learning an instrument or something you like, and it might turn out that you didn't find the most passion, but you will never know if you never try.

Thank you to the company that hired me that day because it brought me to the logistics industry, and I never stepped out.

People today are still asking me how I get to work in this industry for so long and still be full of passion. How did you keep growing and making processes in your position and always go forward?

My answer is straightforward: I do everything to create more value for myself and bring value to people around me; I aim to get better pay by improving myself. I do nothing for money because I know once my value increases, money as part of the rewards will come automatically, and that has been one of the gold rules for my business today as well. Money is meant to serve you, not for you to chase its tail.

There are so many traps that people can fall into when they are desperate for money. Some examples include gambling, crypto investing promises, broker markets, etc. Most of these are scams unless you are a professional in this field, and people can lose a lot of money and fall into debt if they make a wrong decision. It's time to check your life choices to see if you made any decisions because of money as the final goal, nothing more significant than that? Or do you have a bigger purpose behind it? Is money just a tool for you to reach your goal? But are what you are doing now legal? Reasonable? or moral? Is the reason only about yourself? Being selfish? Or is the purpose more significant than yourself? Slow down, take a deep breath, and make a wise choice each time. It is never too late to change!

Focus on growing your value, not money.
The key to being rich is to improve your value! Your value is your wealth!! Being rich doesn't mean you are wealthy; only being valuable and creating value will make you wealthy.

I always take a deep breath and feel how grateful I am. I have a place to live, food to eat, people to love, and people who love me. I can breathe; I am wealthy because I learn, grow, and create value daily. Being grateful makes me feel so rich.

Many people on the planet are rich, but they feel miserable, depressed, lost, upset, lonely…… so many complicated feelings because they can't find their purposes. How much news did you hear about the famous and rich superstars, actors, and actresses who had ended up being broken and depressed? How many sad stories about their divorce and ending up being lonely? People could not find true love or the true meaning of life. Being rich isn't about fame or owning a ridiculous amount of money.

How many of you heard about stories of winning lotteries, and those people ended up fighting with their families simply because of money? Or do they end up spending all their money and become even poorer? They were all real because our life isn't supposed to be purposeless to simply chasing cash and wanting to be rich with no greater purposes than just ourselves.

To find a purpose that is not about money. But use the money to be part of your tools to reach your more immense and unselfish goals. Only that could bring you true happiness.

It would help if you kept learning and growing to be wise and mature enough to know how to increase your value and earn more money simultaneously. But like all of you, the reality at the same time will give me under financial pressure. Like when I got married, I needed to think about buying a house, and when I had my kids, I needed to think about their future. How on earth could I get more pay? Or how could I get treated so specially and differently from my boss or client?

It was my intentional decision. I decided to make an effort to be who I wanted to be.

Six Small Habits help increase your value and build your anti-fear muscles.

I always have been one of the youngest leaders at school or in the workplace. I could always take on the most significant challenges, and people could be amazed by my fearless spirit. Is it because I am super special? No. It was just when I started to fear and worry, and I had to find ways to keep myself out of it. I knew if I didn't, I could not enjoy my life fully or be confident and perform well. My secret is just some tiny habits. According to scientific investigation, it takes only 21 days to build up a person's habit. You can use these tips for 21 days and likely have more anti-fear muscles to live fully and enjoy thoroughly.

I have concluded **Six small habits** you can take away to use in your practical life and build up your anti-fear muscles. I promise you that if you start to manifest them, you will find more joy and fewer worries in your life, and your boss will never say no to increasing your salary; your client or anyone who works with you will enjoy working with you. In other words, you will get wealthier. Because I did, and it worked every single time.

Habit Number One: Being kind.
Always show respect to everyone you know and everything you do. Do well what your position offers but show kindness no matter what you do. Your extraordinary personality will touch people with a bit of kindness.

Being kind is one of the most powerful weapons you could have. I didn't mean that you should spoil people or blindly give more. When someone needs your help, show respect and sympathy by going a bit extra mile and letting them see more hope and love. It requires wisdom and practice to determine the bottom line for you to adjust.

So many famous people in their career would always have someone who showed a small kindness to make them feel worthy and trustworthy. There are Millions of little stories regarding the power of kindness that we can list, but I want you to understand one essential fact: Being kind is not just to others but also yourself.

When you start showing kindness to people, you will receive much more compassion and respect in different ways. Sometimes it may not be from the same person, but you will find your life is full of joy and kindness when you decide to be the one to shine and spread the sunshine. When you are kind to yourself, you will understand that you can forgive yourself quickly and move on. You will give yourself more opportunities to grow and improve every day.

To be kind, you can say or do good things to others. Things you can do, such as pay for a coffee or a meal for someone who needs it. To do volunteer work or help something without expecting any returns. Whenever I couldn't feel many touching things in life, I started to look around for opportunities to be kind.

I once delivered 20 gifts with my daughter to all my neighbours during my 1-hour walk during lockdown legal exercise time. Knowing so many people are suffering from mental health issues, I just wanted them to know they are loved. By doing that, I felt so loved because I knew that if I was thinking of people, there were people who were also thinking of me. I won't mention too much about so many other things I do to spread kindness because these were my hidden joy. However, I found that showing kindness has created my ability to be grateful and loving, it creates power for me to feel more valuable, and it creates more value and capacity in my soul. It connects me and others as one united world.

I heard a story from our Pastor in Lifehouse Church Melbourne about the spread of a kindness story. There was one Starbucks in the USA where a person started to do the test on paying for a coffee for someone, and they found out that more than 20 people paid for the next one. The kindness started to spread again and again.

There is an excellent video about one person who started to help a guy, and then that guy's day lightened up, and he decided to help the other person. The short clip had at least six great things happen just because of a tiny kindness, and the kindness then returns to the person who started it. You can watch it on YouTube by searching: Life Vest Inside – Kindness Boomerang – "One Day" – the link: https://www.youtube.com/watch?v=nwAYpLVyeFU

A small kindness can change the world. The story of Jack Ma, one of the wealthiest people in China, was widely spread. He couldn't reach his destination if he didn't meet an Australian guy willing to show kindness and teach him English for no reason. Because of that, Jack Ma could later manage to go to the USA and learn all the things he needed to become one of the most successful entrepreneurs.

Are you ready to increase your value and change the world? Start with being kind, the quickest and easiest way to start the revolution. You DO NOT need tools to help you be kind; just a decision!

Habit Number Two: Make efforts in every relationship
A relationship is also called a partnership. It needs two sides to participate. Two parts. You cannot have a relationship with yourself. Highly recommend you build up the best relationships with everybody you can connect with. Whether it is your colleagues, boss, or external clients, they are the best' mouths' to sell your values.

When I say: "make efforts in every relationship," I want to highlight Making Efforts. It is not about aiming to delight everyone but aiming to care about everyone around you and do your part. Although some people may not take what you give, you still decide to lead the environment around you, to be the leader that doesn't need a crown but an influencer to shine wherever you are.

I don't mean that you have to make everyone love you. At least try to avoid ruining any relationships in your life. Because every relationship is an excellent opportunity for you to bring success and happiness, you may not get along well with everyone, but at least don't build up any enemies purposely. Within what you can do, purposely cherish every relationship in your life.

Do not purposely let down anybody; instead, lift others as it will lift yourself. One of the secret weapons to my career success is that I make an effort in every relationship and every opportunity when I can see a person. I don't judge them by age, background, culture, or title. By knowing people and spending time with everyone. Only being intentionally willing to make efforts to a relationship can make that relationship shine, no matter what type of relationship.

Something fascinating is that fewer and fewer people are willing to make an effort in a relationship because they would instead focus on feeling better for a short time. But that selfish action doesn't help them to feel better in the long term. A relationship needs mutual efforts to manage; it is a lifelong investment. A married couple can divorce fast if they don't want to make efforts in their marriage. A married couple can become crazily well if they both make efforts in their relationship management.

When I concluded my points, I found an interesting article that concluded 13 facts about how lack of effort could badly impact your relationship.

Lack Of Effort How Badly Impact Your Relationship (13 + Points) – Liesmug

Link: https://www.liesmug.com/lack-of-effort-how-badly-impact-your-relationship/

Let alone all stories outside there in the community; plenty of stories happened in my life too.

My parent's marriage is a typical example. My father didn't want to make an effort to his relationship with my mum when I was younger. That caused so much pain to my mum. My father put all anger and complaints ahead of efforts or responsibilities. They ended up talking about divorce so many times. The marriage was saved when my father was willing to apologize and make up by making efforts. It wasn't perfect marriage as their marriage was pre-arranged. But making efforts made a massive difference to this relationship.

My husband and I don't have many fights, but whenever there was an argument, it was when I didn't see any effort from him, or it would be the other way around, which was no effort from me when I was too focused on something else. When I realized how important it is to make an effort, I would take things seriously and intentionally create romantic time and quality time with my husband.

The same to my parenting life. I remember there were times my daughters were emotionally and very disobedient. After being angry about their behaviour, my husband started to remind me that they wanted me to spend more time with them. Oh dear, that's right, I did not make many efforts during that time. Instead, they became the best kids again when I intentionally made an effort!

Nowadays, everything is related to people and relationships if you work in a workplace or build up your business. Rather than focusing on building up money assets, the wiser thing is to build up your relationships and networks with people around you.

Once you find yourself surrounded by great people and excellent people, no matter if you have money, you no longer feel afraid, and you will feel enough because you still have people to love or to love you.

Habit Number Three: Build up your Willingness.
Be willing to do hard work and show the best attitude.

One of the most important things I sought when I interviewed a delegate for job interviews was their' willingness.' I want to see how much they are willing to and how eager they are. That hunger and burning-fire passion are the keys to making them better candidates than many others. So yes, you must dig out your willingness to accept any challenges. Because extraordinary people are willing to do hard things, take challenges, and have an open mind to open the door to opportunities. Don't be an ordinary person who only likes to seek easy things to do.

We all know that we can teach skills, but we can hardly teach attitude because it is more of a personal choice. If you can learn how to build up your willingness to accept challenges and hard work, you will be more likely to achieve much more significant success in your career or life.

Suppose you are willing to build up your goodwill and show it wherever you go. Opportunities will follow you around. Don't trust when people say: "Oh, they are so lucky!" Nobody is lucky if they have a bad attitude. "A smiley person will always have more luck."

Build the best inner attitude because that shall reflect your willingness to do things, whether willing to help others or take on a complex challenge. Your fantastic attitude can change your life.

Habit Number Four: Be proactive

Be proactive with everything you do and think ahead for your boss, client, or anybody who works with you.

It's similar to an excellent attitude and being willing to. However, being proactive is the reflection and action when you decide to be ready to do things. You would always think ahead of others. Trust me, being proactive makes you a fantastic leader because you would foresee things earlier and be able to handle jobs and manage a team better.

In my two decades of leading, one of the cores I set up for myself and what I do is to be proactive. It helped me grow and dig out so much potential from me.

Imagine you are the boss, and before you ask someone where they are on their tasks, they could come up with what you have thought of or even you have yet to think of. Isn't that amazing if you could stay proactive in what you do? It is related to the will as well. If you are unwilling to, you won't come up with anything proactively.

I always say: either not do or do it with 110% passion. It has the magic to your work and life for anything you do. It will bring you so much growth and joy. To be proactive includes things like finishing things before you are chased; Proactively taking meeting minutes or notes; Thinking ahead of your boss or manager; proactively seeking something to do, and so on. It trains you to be the best version that you don't even expect.

Being proactively ready to accept more enormous challenges can help you get through any challenges quickly. It's not getting prepared because it's already too late when you are still getting ready when the challenge and hardships come already.

If you are pre-ready to do the work, it will always bring you a bonus or salary increase. What if your boss is choosing someone to promote tomorrow? Are you ready? Prepared for any good or trial situation, you may be placed into. Are you prepared to pass the test?

Nowadays, job interviews have become increasingly creative, and some might offer trials to see if you are the right candidate. Rather than pretending to be the person they are looking for, isn't it better that you are already pre-ready for whom they are looking for?

Habit Number Five: Be Consistent.
Keep sending a regular performance report, whether meeting the company's demand or not, as long as it shows your willingness and marks your growth track. Be consistent.

Be consistent with the good things you are doing because that's where you can achieve fulfillment.

It's not the outcome that reflects how different you are. It is consistency.

It's the self-discipline that separates you from ordinary people to the extraordinary.

I had things in life that I only had 3 minutes of heat, and I didn't do anymore because I was trying to experience and find what I would be passionate about. However, I will always be consistent once I find the core and focus on life.

In the last 20 + years, I saw many people who were better than I was in many things and areas, but they stopped growing. They gave up. You could see a brighter future for a person, and you knew that he would become super successful if he could keep up the consistency.

Sadly, most of us are distracted easily, becoming less consistent in doing things.

Work-out and exercise, for example, were outside my routine after I was 18. I was not too fond of it and felt it was a waste of time. Until the day I realized that my health was terrible and my shape wasn't good. I had to do some exercise. That's one of the best decisions I made.

For recent three to four years, I might stop for one or two days maximum, but I would always keep consistent on exercise because it's part of my life, and it's just like eating, drinking, and sleeping. We will die if we don't eat, drink or sleep for a long time. People don't believe until bad things happen or until someone dies because of bad life habits. Why do we always have to see someone dying before we realize we should do the right things?

To keep the consistency, you must find out your 'why.' 'Why do you do it." "What is for.?" The reason must be strong enough for you to keep going, and the reason must be more than just for yourself; your consistency will become more stable.

For example, if you are working for someone in a company and have been performing well and always doing 100% of your job. Still, one day, you don't feel like doing anything, and your mind will tell you to give up and just play a comfortable or selfish team player in your work. Just use 50% or less of your energy or capability.

What decision will you make? One, you will choose to listen to your mind because you don't want to think as you are too tired. But two, you will choose to consider before making a decision and check if you need to keep going. You need to ask yourself, why are you doing the work so hard?

If your answer is to look good in front of others, you will not want to keep going. But most of the time, your real reasons will be either: you always want to do the best and be the best version of yourself, to make a difference, Or you want to keep investing yourself in what you are doing and what you are learning, because it can bring you a brighter future and then alternatively your family and future family, your kids and future kids will benefit from this too. Then you will understand doing something good consistently isn't just for your workplace. It is going to be beneficial to everyone, and you will feel so fulfilled too.

However, don't overburn yourself, which is another thing we should consider, and don't be addicted to overtime working all the time. It needs consistency for you to remind yourself and find ways and things to do to avoid overworking. We have to find balance.

Habit Number Six: Prepared to be worry-less

Always find a backup plan for yourself if you can, but don't worry if you haven't yet. All your previous learnings and efforts have already increased your values to any other organization. I am never worried about my job because I am too focused on my race and on improving my values. And I always believe that whoever gets me to work for them will get more than what they pay me, but if whoever doesn't contact me is their loss.

You must know how to maintain a peaceful heart to achieve the abovementioned goals. Most of the time, if you let the fear of money shortage guide your decision, you can make awful and unwise decisions.

The most helpful thing is an affirmation of self-encourage that I use to calm down my fear of money shortage.

"The money or materials may be changing or can be fewer some days, but

there's one thing in me that I can contribute from various areas, and it is a thing which will never grow less, which is my value. I can use my gifts of value to do anything to raise money." As long as you are strong enough with an unshakable mindset, nothing will be too hard to get through.

Once I started this conversation, it reminded me I still have faith in succeeding. It always turns out that as long as there's a will, there's a way. Nothing is impossible, so I must keep focused and patient.

When you choose to be rich, you also have to raise your standard regularly is essential too, because as time goes by, you are growing, and your capacity is growing as well. If you don't raise your standard, you will lose track, feel down, and feel poor in your spirit.

When I was younger, there was one thing I realized from people in my life and my own experience, as well as when I finished a massive project and achieved a fantastic performance, and then suddenly, I felt down and purposeless for a short time. Or, when I had so many goals to reach and accomplished everything on the list, I suddenly felt something was missing. Yes, that is the new goal and purpose. Our standard is fixed regularly and needs to be raised periodically, too, if we want to be happy continuously because, without stable new growth, we won't be satisfied. Every change of development becomes every irreplaceable property of mine that makes me feel richer every day.

We know so many uncertainties when we do our life, which is why fear is so common, because when you cannot hold or make sure, or you can't see the uncertainties. You will face 'fear.' But now you know your life is always moving on and changing daily. It is essential to keep raising your standard but also give yourself boundaries and know that it is an infinite game and that you are supposed to enjoy the game, not end it earlier.

Keep your rich concept not measured by money or materials but by spiritual growth and experience. The joy and calmness you have are priceless, which is the thing to make you rich! Get rich from today, just with one decision of yours!

Do these affirmation regularly:

"I am strong and resilient. I can get through any difficulties. I can survive no matter whether I have money or not. My value isn't relying on how much I earn but on how much I grow. Failure and falling are part of my success. If I failed in this thing, I could try again. If I try again and it still fails, I will keep trying, and each time I grow more robust and more prosperous with my learnings, not my earnings."

Except for money, the other most significant fear is our health. Do you know our health is our wealth?

I was overweight throughout my childhood and had a low immunization system. Do you remember the 'Skim Milk Please' moment? That was when I started picking up great health habits in my life, not just to look better but feel better with better health. Why don't you walk towards it if you know what is good for you?

I want to share something I do to avoid worries about my future health and age. There is no sugar coating here, but honestly, what you are going to feed into your body is what it will bring. What you decide to do is what you are going to get. If you do not always want to be worried about your health and to be aged so quickly, you need to look at these facts and habits that you must build up to kill your worries. We know some generic things are hard to prevent, but they are still preventable, according to many researchers and authentic experiences.

1. Junk Food has a reason to be called junk. It is not named 'Healthy' but' junk.'
2. There are not many tricks or secrets to losing weight. It is simply "eat less and move more."

3. Gaining weight doesn't have to be fat. Your muscle is heavier than your fat, and eating more sometimes won't make you look chubbier if you know how to eat smartly and do work-out.
4. Better body shape looks more expensive than expensive clothes, but you do not need to be the same size as others. All sizes are ok as long as your body functions well.
5. Do not be lazy and accept your current status just because you persuaded yourself you are content. Being too comfortable can blind you from seeing the truth. If you have any worries about how you look, face them and start to change your habits, and you will get there.
6. We can buy a bed, but we cannot buy good sleep; we can buy food but not good health; we can buy expensive clothes, but we cannot buy better shapes. Someone may say: We can do surgery. Yes, you can, but you cannot buy a lifelong guarantee that it won't come back if you don't try to maintain your own body. The only lifelong security is your self-determination and your commitment to yourself.
7. The other thing is that everyone knows that one day we shall die physically. In Christianity, if you believe in Jesus, who died on the cross for you and forgiven all your sins, your soul will go to heaven. But even before we go to heaven, we cannot prevent being aged. Everybody believes to be young and energetic is excellent.

To be aged doesn't mean we are growing older in our spirit. We can always maintain a young and energetic spirit and attitude to live our life. I always imagine myself still wearing lots of colours and fashions at the age of 90 and dancing like a kid, which would be fantastic.

To be fearless doesn't mean you won't have any more fear in your life. Some reasonable fears help us avoid danger and protect ourselves.

For example, when you see a bad guy running to get you, fear will alert you to run. We must decide to lead our worry, not let our fear rule us. Please turn off the false alarm so we can see the actual warning clearly and take advantage of using the alarm.

If we always expect to be Fear-free, we will be poorly bothered because our expectations will bring us more fear and anger. The best medicine to conquer your unnecessary fear is: To trust and to believe, which is your faith. In other words, don't only believe what you see, but trust what you don't see, your future, and that you are meant to do bigger things and fulfill great purposes. It may not happen in one or two days, but you will get there if you keep trusting and believing that good things will always happen sooner or later.

Start to switch off the false fear alarm system today, keep trying new things, and believe in yourself. You will meet the most confident self of you.

CHAPTER SIX

Joyful Leadership Language.

Lead to speak powerfully.

R*ather than choose to make excuses, wisely choose your leadership language.*

First, as a leader, please watch out for Your Language (Your Words). We can speak so many words each day, but do we pick up the wise languages to talk about? I highly doubt it! When I am doing a speech and drafting something, I think about it more carefully before saying it. But if I am just talking to someone, the processing time is much shorter so I may not pay much attention anymore.

We all know the magic of skillful communication, and especially if you know how to effectively communicate with a person by standing on their point of view, you will find lots of favour. A small tongue of ours is powerful but also dangerous. If we don't know how to manage or use it properly, it can also set fire and cause many issues. Oh, it will also bring you opportunities to make excuses if you don't pick your words wisely.

Bad communication can ruin someone's life. I read an article that talks about four historical communication failures that could have been prevented here: https://www.beekeeper.io/blog/4-historical-communication-failures-prevented-beekeeper/

One of the sad stories from there was:

QUOTE:
Battle of Marathon
Everyone knows that a marathon race is 26.2 miles, but not everyone knows how that came to be. The Greek myth goes that Philippides, a messenger, was sent from the Battle of Marathon to announce the Persians had been defeated. The problem was he ran the entire distance, and when he made it to the Greek assembly he was only able to say, "We are winners!" before collapsing to the floor and dying.

Poor Philippides could have been saved with a simple internal communications app letting his countrymen in the assembly know of Greece's victory. Then again, we wouldn't have what we know as a marathon today, so Philippides' sacrifice was more significant than he'll ever know.
UNQUOTE

In the other words, a good communication can change the world. How many great speeches that changed history? Who hasn't heard and been touched by Martin Luther King's "I have a dream" speech? The other funny example: One expert on leadership, Nick Morgan, interviewed by the Public Affairs Council, says, "when he spoke, the room came alive. The energy was tremendous. But when Hillary spoke...all the energy left the room." Why TED Talk becomes so popular and famous? There is strength in words when you can speak powerfully. I believe powerful words can bring light and healing. Why are there so many leaders in the world who don't know how to solve a problem but have the power to communicate and bring the right people to solve problems? As a leader, learning how to speak powerfully is a must.

There are so many academic courses you can pay for and learn online about effective communication. I never took any lessons about it, but I read articles, watched helpful information, and, most importantly, learned much from my experience of practicing in real life.

One main thing is from day one when I was representing the company, despite my position or title, every email I started with **'We' rather than 'I.'** Because I knew that I am always part of all and we are one, this excellent leadership language gave me power and led me always think of ways rather than excuses. When I said 'I,' if I couldn't do something, I could blame others in my team or the company. When I said 'we,' there was no one I could complain to anymore. It stimulated so much more superpowers and leadership energy in me.

I don't just say 'we' in my workplace; I also say it in my family. Whatever I do, I don't want to take credit for myself, and I always want to do things on behalf of us all. This habit brought so much leadership power to how I react or handle things.

What we say comes from what we think and will affect our actions. What we say will also affect what we believe. In short, if we have a thought, we either need to do it or fix what we think if that's not something we should say or do. You must lead these crucial areas and start from somewhere. The effective way is to fix what we think; what we believe will change what we say and reflect what we do.

Are you all familiar with these situations? Fights, quarriers, or even killings were caused by some unnecessary words one person said. The scariest part is that sometimes many of these languages from people were subconscious, which means they didn't even think about what they said. But it potentially brought hard feelings and harm to the others listening. Of course, we cannot scare or care too much if we want to say something out of good purpose and not try to attack people. The point here is that we need to Watch out for the language we speak.

Many words in this world have lost their true meanings and are significantly misused by many of us! I want to highlight some of them for you to do your leadership responsibilities and self-check!

The below tips could help you significantly fix your leadership language:

TIP ONE: Failure VS Setback & redirection

We can easily say things like: "I failed." "I failed my test." "I failed to manage my business!"

Failure is never a negative thing; it is a process to success and part of success. A leader will speak of failure as a setback and redirection. I strongly recommend everyone in the world start to treat it with a positive word!

When failure comes, it is the setback that you need time to fix and re-look at what you did and what you could do better! And it is the time for you to find the redirection because life is always a going-on journey. It will always provide new challenges. Redirecting the experience helps you achieve much better things than ever!

We must understand that life isn't what we think it will be. It is always unpredictable, so we will always face setbacks and redirections. But we must realize that failure only happens when you agree with it. The moment you never give up fighting, you will never fail.

So, whenever you want to say words like *I failed, I am a failure!* Please change your comments to: *'I am failing, and I am facing a setback, but yeah, I am facing a redirection!'* Keep practicing, and it will bring a transformational change in your life. It will not allow you to find excuses not to keep trying and looking forward to a new challenge because the game is never over.

TIP TWO: Be lazy VS Be purposeless
I always hear people say that they are lazy, which shocked me. The problem is that those who said they were lazy are doing loads of business or other things. They ignore their contributions and don't fill themselves with more gratefulness and self-love. Of course, they lack motivation when saying that they are lazy. Are you doing the same thing?

I understand that you may have days when you don't feel like doing much, but it doesn't mean you are lazy. You need to find out where your passion lies and pick it up. The purpose shall then lead you to motivation and then to action.

However, when you need to take a day off or sometimes to recharge yourself, your minds start to tell you that you are lazy, and then you believe you are. Your behaviours begin to show and cooperate with what you say about yourself. Remember that we will only become who we believe we are. If your mind thinks you are lazy, you will become sluggish. To stop it, you must start by using your leadership language.

Being lazy and less motivated is different.

Most of the time, you think you were lazy just because you lost your passion; you couldn't find why you existed and what you wanted to achieve; in short – you are purposeless. So, when you feel down or tired, change your leadership language to: "I have been less motivated recently, and I am going to find out my motivation." "I am in a slow season, but I will find my speed soon." "I am in a low valley but climbing up to the mountain one day." Stop saying that you are lazy, but instead, start to appreciate your efforts and find ways to bring back your passion, motivation, faith, confidence, and belief in yourself!

Practice this every day! Whenever you think you are 'lazy,' say to yourself: 'I lack purpose, and I am going to find out where my purpose is." it will help you find out your passion and purpose for doing what you do.

Here are some tips that could help you gradually transform from being purposeless to purposeful. Everything starts from the first step. You decide which ways you prefer because everyone is different and has a unique way of transforming. Still, I guarantee you that if you intentionally step out to do things from this list and commit to them. You will see transformation in life. I tried each of them, and they all worked.

Magical Small Habit Lists to create an energetic and highly self-disciplined day:

1. Set up an alarm with a motivational note.
Set up an alarm and put things you need to do the following day on the notes next to the notice.

If you want to wake up earlier the following day, always set the alarm. But in case you don't think it's necessary to wake up in time, get anything that can remind you and motivate you as a note that you can see the very first when you wake up.

Some things that motivated me are Bible Study and Workout. This is also why I would put all my Workout clothes next to my bed, reachable within 2 seconds, a reachable place that doesn't allow excuses to give up doing what I need to do.

2. Start your day with a big glass of water.
I have this great habit of drinking a whole glass of water every morning. It helps me to feel refreshed and energetic. It clears my body and pushes all junk from my body after a good sleep. God creates water for all nature, including humans. Water is the best drink for us.

3. Start your day with a great healthy green drink.
I always make my green drink every morning. The latest one I made was combined with cucumber, celery, green apple, and anything I'd like to add that morning. I tried ginger, lemon, banana, watermelon, bitter

melon, or carrots. Each of them has a different function and significant benefits to our body. I could spend another hour talking about each great thing and its taste, but they taste great and benefit our bodies.

A day starting with green gives me so much comfort that even though I may not be able to eat vegetables in the daytime, my body has enough quota to fight the day. Besides, it helps so much with my immunization system. Since I started this habit, I have rarely gotten sick. The max sickness I got was only three times in the last ten years, including the COVID time.

4. Start your day with something.

If you can hardly wake up, the easier way is to move your steps to the bathroom – I believe everyone needs it in the morning, right?

I am very good at waking up early, but there were times before when I was exhausted, and I didn't want to wake up earlier, so I would go back to sleep. The more I told myself I was tired and didn't want to get up, the harder I could get up. Then I found out a trick. It worked well. I just went to the bathroom directly once the alarm rang, and as time passed, I started to feel less sleepy and more awake when I sat on the toilet bowl.

If you can hardly wake up, and if you can do something, push yourself to start setting up your bed. Set-up your bed is small, but it brings so much big help to your life. If you have a hard day, go and set up your bed; If you lose confidence, go and set up your bed; If you don't know what to do, go and set up your bed. Why? Set-up your bed to start your day will bring you confidence and an outstanding achievement about yourself that if you can do one thing well, you can do anything well.

When I was in the corporate workplace, people were coming and guiding staff about tidying up our work desks and office place, and it has the same philosophy. Being tidy can change your life. Suggest you check out Marie Kondo, a Japanese organizing consultant, author, and

TV presenter. Kondo has written four books on organizing, which have collectively sold millions of copies worldwide. Her books have been translated from Japanese into several languages, and her book *The Life-Changing Magic of Tidying Up* (2011) has been published in more than 30 countries.

5. Start your day with hard things. I highly recommend Workout.

I like to start my day with hard things. I heard stories about Tony Robins, who would do the cold shower every morning, and that's a thing. But I'd choose to do the Workout. As a mum and full-time business owner, it's not likely for me to go to the Gym because that could be too luxurious for me timewise. So, I choose to use YouTube and do the Workout.

Why Workout? There are too many benefits that you can find online from experts. I tried, then what I discovered that benefited me the most was an incredible improvement in so many areas of my life: controlling my weight, improving my body shape, improving my mental health and keeping up positive thinking, improving my sleep, and not joking, it improves sexual health too.

I hated walking or running because I felt my time was precious for something else, and I hated feeling the pain during Workouts. I would never think that I could or love to do Workouts.

I was wrong. Anybody can do a workout, and nobody cannot be trained. I always believed that I was born fat or baby fat from my DNA, and I don't have any sports DNA in me, but there were all excuses, and they were all wrong.

If you saw my photos a long time ago, a few years ago compared to now, before and after the Workout. You could already see a huge difference. I found it extremely hard initially, and I didn't believe I could. But, surprisingly, I started by doing seven-minute daily workouts to 10 to 20, then 30 minutes, and then I wanted more.

A friend told me a real story: he had a super big friend, his size was crazily big, and he could not do anything properly anymore because he was too fat. He lost all the motivation to exercise. But one thing my friend asked him to do saved this guy's life. He asked him to do ten plus ten plus 10. Every morning, when he wakes up, before doing anything else,

he starts by doing 10 Sit-ups, ten push-ups, and 10 Squats. One month later, when my friend saw this guy, he was amazed. He lost so much weight by simply doing these. Why?

The ten plus ten plus ten is just a starting point; everything is hard when you get started, but once you get into it, your body will crave more, and it becomes easier when you begin to do more.

It is the same in my experience. I ended up consistently doing Workout for almost three years. Little by little, I saw transformations in all areas of my life. Thus, you don't need to be worried. If the big fat guy and I can do it, so can you. Just get started small, and you will see a great result in life. An ocean starts from one drop of water.

6. *Forget how you look.*

Forgetting how I look is a great habit I have. Because when I remember my look, there will be two possibilities.

One, I am too distracted by how beautiful I look and forget about the inside beauty and the efforts I need to make.

Or two, I am too distracted by comparison, will easily focus more on how others look better than I am, and lose track of my confidence and life journey.

In my life, I always forget about how I look, and instead, I focus on how I want to become and who I believe I will become. I focus on my identity. Write down my identity and focus on going for it.

I remember I was only an ordinary worker who worked for some companies two years ago. I wrote down my target of identity that I believed I would become. I wrote down 'author,' 'speaker,' a 'change-maker,' and an 'entrepreneur.' Everything I wrote down just became a reality in two years.

The truth is that you have everything in you. You have all you need in you. That is your belief. Forget about how you look today, write down who you believe you should be. Then go for it! You will thank me because I know you can do it.

The confident look is more beautiful! You will see amazing things happen as long as you believe and stay focused on your journey.

7. *Look at your naked self in the mirror*

One of the things I suggest – if you cannot find the motivation to exercise- is to look at your naked body in the mirror. I know this might sound weird, but to do this is first to allow yourself to accept yourself entirely; Second, to keep yourself aware of the status of your body so that you can find the need to do more exercises.

Most of us will always want to improve our appearance because we all want to be healthy and fit. **"No pain, no gain"** equals **"Yes pain, yes gain."** If we're going to achieve results, we always can as long as we take action.

There are many inspirational people you can search for and give yourself fewer excuses but more motivation. Check out an article: 17 Super Fit Older People Who Can Kick Your Ass – Pulptastic

Link: https://pulptastic.com/seniors-you-shouldn't-mess-with/

There is no reason others can do it but you can't. It's all about your determination and your motivation.

TIP THREE: Content VS Settled

Being content means you are grateful for what you have right now, which brings you great joy. Whether you achieved your final goals or not, you enjoy this moment! It doesn't mean that you will settle.

'Being settled' means you decide not to chase anything anymore, which is dangerous. Because life never stops growing and moving on, **we shall be raised by our standards if we don't raise our standards.** It will teach us more painful lessons to handle unexpected challenges or painful experiences.

A settled person can live in a vibrant place lacking nothing materially but be very miserable, but there is no more growth because he has no more intention to grow and wants to live in his comfort zone. Without growth, there is no joy.

A content person can live a poor life without being lack of materials but still be happy. But this person will never stop fighting and learning to grow. He can continually accept new challenges and leave his comfort zone.

I have never settled down, but I am constantly content and grateful. To be truly fulfilled, you must know the difference and take the lead to be pleased but not settled!

Change your leadership language to: "I am content and grateful, but I will never be settled."

TIP FOUR: New VS Start

"Well, you are just the new staff here; I have been here for a long time."

"Oh, are you new here? You need to learn more."

"You are too new to handle this task."

"You are just a new mum, and you know nothing."

"You are still new; mind your gap, ok?"

"You are younger than us; how will you manage us?"

"You came later than us. You will not get a promotion earlier than us."

How many of you are judged by people because you are new to some area or something? You are facing judgment from many people because they DON'T KNOW you and consider you as 'New' and a 'beginner.'

They see you as one of their previous 'disappointment experiences' because 'they don't know,' so they choose not to believe in you and decide to doubt and judge you instead. They thought you were nothing special.

Do you have the exact moment? Do you sometimes feel that other bigger guys are looking down upon you? Or do clients judge you because you are not as big as the competitors? But if you think more about it, is it really 'bigger' is 'better'? The more, the merrier. Or is it more about 'Quality'?

You don't have to prove to them because the truth will reveal itself over time. Your success and your work will tell the truth.

The key is not how others see you but how you see yourself! Let me ask you! Aren't all current successful or big companies started from 'New' and 'Beginning'? Weren't you started from zero for all your business too? How about when you started as a baby to now as an adult? See how far you have been reaching?

Being new to something doesn't mean being unqualified. Being fresh for something brings more passion and quick learning. In my career, I always treat myself as the 'new' to new challenges. Only remaining a hungry and teachable heart could help us to grow. And everyone, no matter how long they are working in their positions, always has 'new things they didn't handle before, but why could they take it well and survive?

I have always been a leader at school or in the workplace, and I was always the youngest one, and there are always people who could have more life experiences than I have. How could I be the leader to resolve so many problems? How could I feel I could lead?

Well, this is my secret. The secret to keeping growing and learning is that I keep myself as a new beginner every day with the hunger to increase and improve. The secret to leading my team is knowing that we are equal, just playing different roles in the company, as we are a team. The secret to resolving 'new' challenges is 'confidence and trust' by knowing that even though I may not fix this perfectly, I will only create a new learning experience. Most of the time, that calm and peaceful heart and thoughts work out the magic.

I got good news for you today, no matter if you struggle to be new in any area. Being a leader isn't about knowing everything but being in charge of your people to know more and shine. In other words, you help people dig out the best of themselves and learn from them while they are growing and learning from you. It is not about how long or how new you are. What a wonderful thing to lead a team with a win-win result!

Change your leadership language to: "I am new, but I have started, and that means I am one step closer to my goal each time." "I am new to something good, which means I am hungrier to learn more things more efficiently." "I am new to this area, but I believe I can bring more inspiration, passion, and influence on people around me, particularly during the honeymoon starting period."

TIP FIVE: Past Failure DO NOT lead Your Future.
We always use our past experiences to judge our future. So, we say things like these to reflect our past in our language: "I am not sure because I didn't do it before." "I will never be able to do it because I tried before, and it didn't work." "I am sick of it." "It never happened before, and I don't think it will happen now."

Our minds will always automatically tell us if we will have a great future, relying on what we did in the past and our past experiences. Please do not mix 'past' and the 'future.' **Our future depends on what we believe about it, what we want for it, and why we want it.** If our past defines our future, please google, and search to see how there can be so many successful people who had a very turbulent history.

For example, Jack Ma, again a good example, is one of the wealthiest men who used to own Alibaba. He failed school when he was younger and got rejected many times before he started to succeed. Stephen King, a famous American horror author, was just a Janitor, and one of his most successful books 'Carrie' was rejected by 30 publishers before he succeeded. Robert Downey Jr, our favourite 'Iron Man in Marvel's Avengers movies series, was addicted to drugs and alcohol. How about Tony Robbins, a successful American top-seller author, coach, and speaker? He had an immensely struggling childhood.

How about Joyce Meyer? American Charismatic Christian author, speaker? She has written 300+ books, and her show and books are widely translated into hundreds of countries, but she had a very tough past. She suffered from her dad's sexual abuse and struggled financially in the earlier days before she succeeded. There are so many more stories we can tell. These examples reflect that 'your past does not define 'your future. So, take out the words you mentioned that referred to the past to define what you can achieve in the future. Do not set up your limits because of your old experience when it comes to 'belief.' Everyone and everything can change.

I worked for a few companies and have helped the company grow as much as possible, no matter where I go. Imagine if I carried my previous experience when trying to sell toys in the street as my first experience but ended up becoming a failure story that my sister has always been laughing at me. I doubted myself every day and was questioned by everyone that nobody thought I could be a businesswoman. If I carried the belief based on any of my experiences to decide my future, I would never be able to become who I am today.

I started my own business only not long ago. It is swiftly well-known and recognized by people in a short time. If I doubt that my previous experience isn't what I am strictly going to do, or if I bring any of my past failing experiences with me, I will never be courageous enough to start my business.

When I started my business, I decided to throw away my past failure and doubts. In the beginning, it was also very hard, and I faced many failures, such as trusting the wrong person, being too generous to somebody, or missed opportunities to charge more. I learned so many lessons, and I am still learning. However, when I decide to focus on something and to achieve something, such as my business goals, I choose to see its future on where I am with the goal achieved, and I choose not to see the barriers because I know that when barriers come, I can always handle them.

As long as there's a will, there is a way. Our vision and the 'why' behind it will lead us to the best places. People may laugh at you or feel that your dream is unrealistic. Like Forest Gump in the old movie, keep running your vision, let them laugh, and let them ignore you until the day they are amazed!

100% of the successful people had tough times, and they were like every one of us! Doubts! Setbacks! But one thing in common, they BELIEVE, they DO, and they NEVER QUIT! We know we are playing an infinite game, and the game won't be over if we don't stop, and we will always stand up and get up and keep going!!

To all business owners or starters!! To whoever is struggling, keep going!! You decide to be who you are! If you don't have many audiences, be your audience because everyone will come and watch your show one day. Because you are too busy to live in others' shows. Your show may start a bit late, but it is always running and never stops.

To change your leadership language is to say things like: "I didn't do it before, but I know I can do it in the future." "I will never stop trying to do it because I believe I can" "I believe I can." "I tried, but it didn't work, but it doesn't mean it won't work in the future unless I try enough and in different ways." "What I experienced in the past doesn't have authority to define my future; my future is based on my belief." "I believe in my future!"

TIP SIX: Too late VS Get Started!
Did you always hear the opposite voice when you wanted to do something that you thought you should have started earlier?

Never too late to start! KFC owner who started KFC at the age of 65.

Ray Croc was 52 when he first opened his first McDonald's franchise.

Ernestine Shepherd, the world's oldest female bodybuilder, started working out at the ripe age of 56.

There are so many more examples we can find. But the key is you will have to believe and admit it's never too late. Rather than saying, TOO LATE, why not say: "Let's get started!"

A leader knows 'too late' is a lie.

Don't say: "No, I am too old for this!" Let's say: "Yes, I start late, but at least I get started! That means one big first step!"

Don't say: "No way, too late for me to start that business; people already had one!" Let's say: "Let's do it! I can always start something and create new things because nobody is the same."

Don't say: "It's too late for me, and I never prepared it before!" Let's say: "It's great at least I can start to prepare now, and I could have been the one who started this thing the latest, but probably the best!"

Use the leadership languages I listed above and use them not just to speak to yourself but to the people around you. You will find light and shining sparkles in your life and the people who live in your life.

You may say: What on earth should we measure our daily words if we have to use all words carefully? Our life will be so stressful and too challenging. But it is elementary and straightforward.

There are a few questions for you to ask yourself so that you can measure before you say it:

1. Is it necessary?
2. Is it kind?
3. Is it helpful?

Powerful words are great, but it isn't enough because all transformations only happen through action. 'Do it!' In the next chapter, we will find a way to empower ourselves to do things intentionally and proactively.

CHAPTER SEVEN

Joyful Leadership Power.

Lead to finish strong.

Actions speak louder than words and thoughts; knowledge is not power if you don't apply it to life; Knowledge is only powerful until you light up the fire. Leadership isn't decisive unless you take action.

Many prefer to speak, and few choose to listen appropriately.

Many prefer to think, and few choose to do it appropriately.

Many prefer to do, and few choose to think appropriately.

Will you choose to do it after good thinking and talking? Clean up the barriers along the way?

It is easy to fall in love, but it is hard to get along and live together.

It is easy to start a relationship or something, but it is hard to get to the end. How can we start well and finish well?

Before we go through how to light up our joyful leadership power and lead to finish strong, we must spend some time knowing about ourselves first. Each of us is different, and we all have different personalities.

There are plenty of magnetic personality tests you can do online for free if you want. One of the best is Free Personality Test | . 16Personalities Link: https://www.16personalities.com/free-personality-test

Remember, even though these tests are helpful, and my conclusion can be practical, we are still different because of our diverse backgrounds, culture, experience, etc. These are just for guidance. Most importantly, you get the critical takeaway about the areas you need to improve to practically transform your life and others' life.

However, to make it easier for you, I concluded some fascinating facts differently according to my own life experience. They are **the three Groups of Major Personalities.**

The first big group is the T group – Thinking.

Those who always think and overthink do not even talk or speak about it, or they always think but do nothing about it—just an empty thought.

T groups are great listeners, they may have lots of great ideas and wisdom, but because they have no intention to put thoughts to practice through action, they will hold them until the ideas die. The views will stay as thoughts forever. It becomes useless as it is only just a thought in their minds.

This group may have billions of fancy ideas and think they are wise and super intelligent, but nothing has changed or happened in their life because they keep thinking and enjoying the thoughts in their minds. Sometimes they might stick their mind with frustrations by overthinking, and then they feel helpless and very venerable just because they haven't even moved their first step.

I met people who rarely talk or share their ideas and don't do many actions, but they think a lot all day. You may be familiar with that when you have something done successfully, and someone would say: I had that idea, or I knew my opinion would work. The problem with the T group is that as they don't even talk about it, share it with someone, or manifest it in life, and the ideas will be forgotten and wholly wasted. These are the typical T group.

The second group is – the S group. Speaking.
Those who always speak for everything in their mind won't have time to process if it's wiser to say it later or not. They don't usually make much effort to filter their words before they speak. One of the bad habits is that they may start to tell everyone about something that hasn't even been created.

The good thing about that is that 'speaking ahead of doing' could bring them pressure, and it can either become a negative or positive power to pull them to do it.

But in general, typical S-group people never stop talking. Speaking is their strength, making them great speakers if their words are appropriate. But the other problem about S Group is that they may hardly stop saying and sometimes they would bring you all the details you don't need or want to know when you are just expecting some short and sweet information.

S group people also have a similar issue as the T Group because they are too busy speaking to listen, plan and do. They may also end up over-promising too many things, as they may even need to remember what they said another time.

The third group is – The A group. Actions.
A group is people who will do it whenever they hear or think of something. They keep trying and keep doing until they find what they want and what they need.

The exceptionally A group can keep trying and doing everything, but sometimes they may lose focus because if you are busy doing everything, you will end up doing nothing.

So many people have goals, but only some achieve everything they want. Because our time is limited. What we invest is what we get. For A group, if they go exceptionally to do everything, they may achieve nothing. Action is excellent, and moving to the first step is great, but if we don't balance thinking (planning wisely) and speaking (communicating effectively), A group can also fail.

You should check which group you belong to more. You don't need a professional test to find out. If you are willing to sit and think, you know yourself more than others see about you. There's no secret that you don't know about yourself. Or you can ask a trustworthy friend to find out which group you belong to more.

Can you then select the excellent part of the T and S groups and put them into A group which is the action? You can think and learn so many things, and you can read and listen to so many good tips, but if you don't start to put them into practice and keep trying again and again in your life, you won't get the result that you are expecting to have. If you can speak so many times and communicate well, but if your actions don't align with your words, do you think people will listen to you?

Let's talk more about those non-extremely ones in A group, which are the healthy ones.

Healthy A group of people would always put their thoughts and words into action. It speaks louder than words.

Many good leaders have the symbol of A – actions. Therefore, many things will get done and achieved. If they fail, they will re-direct and do it again until they achieve success.

If you are more like the T group, one of the biggest traps you need to avoid is 'overthinking.' Because T Group, most likely, may always be busy with thinking and planning but have little time to get started. If you are T Group,

If you are more like the S group, one of the fascinating things I find in my real life is that many of the leaders in the corporate world are excellent S Group speakers. However, many of them are more speakers than doers. That is why we can balance speaking, thinking, and action at the same time. The leadership power is going to be lit up on fire.

I am sure everyone wants to live to the best versions of themselves and use the most of their inner power and talents. So, I have a piece of good news for you. The good part is that we all have these three groups in us. It is just a decision to wisely manage our time of these elements in us, to empower ourselves more by manifesting them in the best ways to serve us.

Ideally, we should all be in the A group (not the extreme one) and grab all the needed strength from T and S groups. My suggestion for everything you do will be 20% time thinking, getting prepared (To get your mind ready), 20% time speaking (keep regular reminding through speaking and declaring,) and 60% time doing. Continuous trying and doing, as well as experiencing, can help you gain more ideas for your thoughts and then help you more with your new words of speaking, speaking with wisdom and experience. Unless you are a speaker and a preacher, it will be counted into the 'doing category' because you are practicing, which is your action.

How can we take action, and how can we finish well?

Is it incredible that you can say something that you are going to do, but the most powerful voice comes from the outcome, and that's when you finish well?

As you may know, my strength is to 'turn ideas into reality.' So here are the three secret steps we should look at to get our dreams fulfilled, and then our goals will become 'things to be achieved instead of just' dreams in mind.'

Three Steps:

- **Get started and use the Magic of small.**
- **Enjoy the process**
- **Finish strong**

The first step is to **get started and use the Magic of small.**

To get started, we have to understand the Magic of small.

When we start something, we always want to do something big. Or we haven't learned how to stand up yet, and we would always want to try to run. There's one thing that we know but always choose to ignore the Magic of small. We think to be more significant is more powerful.

But small is so important. Everything started from small.

Every big business started from small.

Companies like Amazon, Apple, Disney, and Google started in small garages. They were all small, but they kept focusing on the small things and continued going on, which helped them achieve who they are today.

Every successful person starts from the small step.

Every significant achievement started from small achievements. Yahoo chairman Maynard, if you google about him. He got an internship as a security guard at IBM first. Sometimes the Magic of small is that you just need to move your first faithful step, and more opportunities will flow to you to keep seizing. I would not be as confident as I am today if I hadn't made many small achievements. I know that doing everything small nicely can give me the capacity and capability to handle more important things.

I heard a story from my father about the military coaching that everyone has to set up their bed perfectly every morning, and if they don't, they will be punished. You will be surprised at why they do that. Their focus is a more significant thing, not these silly small things. But they have learned that if they cannot even do a small something well, they cannot do anything more significant. It is why so many people start to practice small habits and see the immense transformation in life as time goes by.

Every big habit is built up from tiny patterns. So many people choose to spend time watching Netflix or playing PS4 games that they don't know these small things are taking away their precious time in life. So, deciding what small things you spend time with are crucial.

My daughter Sze started loving to read when she was not even 2. The time we spent with her, even though it was only 5-10 minutes each day, soon built up her hobby and habit of reading. By age 4, she was ready to go to school because she knew so many words. I then realized that she had been reading hundreds of books. Now, it's more than thousands of books as she never skips any day, just because she loves it and the tiny thing has become part of her. I am so thankful I did the small thing when she was younger, as I am already too busy to read with her or guide her now.

Every big guy you see was born into a small family. We were all small when we were babies and kids, but nothing can stop us from growing because being small can be powerful.

Every famous star becomes famous by starting to play a small role.

Mother Teresa didn't think she could make such a huge impact. All she was trying to do was do those small things. Spread love through all small things as possible.

If you don't think 'small is power, check out the airplane stopper, and see how small it is compared to the airplane itself. If you don't think 'small is powerful,' check the ants and see how many times heavier than their body weight they could carry.

How about the seed? When you planted it, it was so small, but how on earth could it grow into a giant tree and grow so many fruits too? How about you and me? Were we born as big as we are now? Were we born as capable and intelligent as we are now? No. We all started from being small.

If you don't think 'small is power, how can we have the Olympic champions today? Were they just born to be a champion, or were they trained with small daily habits to become a champion? How about the Paralympics athletes? Small habits are essential, bringing the Magic to your big success.

So, remember to get it started, do not overthink, and start with the small things.

The second step is to **enjoy the process.**

How can you expect to finish well if you don't enjoy the process?

It took me a long time to understand what living now means. If I think about getting the outcome earlier and quickly whenever I do something, I cannot enjoy the process because all I have will be anxiety and worries.

If we live but worry about tomorrow, I cannot enjoy today and the process. Living today means I genuinely enjoy now by knowing that my future is bright and that good things are waiting for me.

My older daughter always wanted a little sister, so she even prayed and prayed, and then she got a younger sister. She was so thrilled and enjoyed that cute and warm cuddles. Then she realized that the little sister was too little and that she couldn't play with her or understand her. So, she started wishing the younger sister could grow up quickly. Then the younger sister grew up and was no longer a little round ball. You could move around and play around. She has her ideas, her temper, and her own choice. They could finally play together with something the younger one could understand, but one day, when my older one saw the other cute baby around, she said: "too cute, and I wish you could have another baby." See, it isn't that we don't have something; there are things we have, but we always look at what we don't have that will ruin our ability to enjoy the process.

It was a huge life-changing decision when you decided to enjoy the process. When I started my own business, it was not easy at all. So many setbacks, hardships, pains, and problems. These are all the processes that re-direct me to be stronger and to learn more. I realized that if this was easy, everybody else could have done it. Isn't that wonderful to accept a challenge, make a difference, and achieve? When I decided to enjoy my process, it made a huge difference that I could then keep achieving more without burning out. Things like celebrating each small milestone gave me energy and encouragement.

A frank story was shared when we came from Hong Kong to Australia; the struggle was real. It wasn't material-wise. It was the cultural conflict. Even though I adapted to the new environment quickly, there were still things that took me time to get used to. We love the place and people, but we could hardly agree with their life speed sometimes. If anyone knows about people from Hong Kong, probably from most Asian countries, that people got up early and started working and working long hours and always put work as an essential part of life. Hard-working is a symbol of Asian culture, especially in China, where I could tell. Don't get me wrong, there will be 'slow' personalities in Asia too. As mentioned, we are all humans, and there are differences and similarities. However, we must admit that different countries and cultures bring different styles. Every culture has its shining point.

Back to the story, I was so shocked when I saw some people could check their email only twice a day, and their productivities were so low. Something that I used to deal with in half an hour or shorter, they can wait and hold it until the next day, week, or month. Even when we rang someone to get answers for something, the efficiency was always so low. I was struggling with all the waiting, and I had to learn how to drive people to do and finish things earlier and more quickly. I had to be super skillful because I did not want to offend anybody. Sometimes I could be so frustrated and angry with the situation that I could not control or change it.

When you cannot change things outside, you must change something inside you. With so many struggles, I had to find better ways to live because I did not want to lose my joy and I still want to enjoy my life. So, I started to make a rule in my life: 'To enjoy the process.' When I began facilitating that rule, my perspective started to change. When my view started to change, I began to change myself. Our inside mind reflects what we would choose and do.

There was once the very first time I appeared in the kitchen area of our office. I felt so uncomfortable because my mind reminded me how much work I needed to do, and I shouldn't be stopping here and wasting my time. I ignored that noise the first time; I only spent 5 minutes, then returned to my desk. Then 10 minutes next time. I still did more work than talking or resting in the kitchen. But the difference is that I started to find a balance between 'working hard' and 'stopping to smell the roses.'

I was reminded that one of the reasons why I decided to move to Australia was that I wanted to have a more balanced family life. In Hong Kong, I had to spend so much on traffic and could hardly find time to be with my family. I realized I could still work very hard, but in the meantime, stop and rest at the right time. I started to appreciate more and more and admire people who take things slowly but also dig more profoundly because they have a clearer mind to think before doing. There is no fixed formula for everyone because only you know what your balanced time management is to let you enjoy the process. I still work very hard because it gives me fulfillment and joy, but I also plan necessary breaks into my schedule because if I don't do it, I will skip the gap and keep going.

To people outside there like me, if you don't know how to rest and enjoy the process, I want you to know these stories. I heard many real-life stories that give me big hits and reminders, but I will share some with you here.

One is a friend whose sister-in-law was a young CEO, and she was very successful in her career but ended up depressed because of too much pressure. She had a miscarriage several times and decided to resign from her business and focus on being a housewife and producing her babies.

The other is a friend from China who has run his company for 10-15 years, and he became a billionaire, and when everyone envies what he has achieved. The sad story revealed his daughter was not getting much attention from her parent because she got so much money to spend without any of her efforts. She was obsessed with drugs and went out with so many bad friends who were very much like her we call 'The Rich second generation." Choosing friends who could bring you a positive impact instead of a bad one is important. So, because of that, they did many silly things simply because they wanted short-term fun. It was a disaster. It took the friend a long time to involve and fix the situation. He still could not return to the childhood he was supposed to spend with his daughter.

One of my friend's friends owned a successful and profitable business but had an autistic son. The couple was very hard-working but ignored their child, which became a long-term problem they had to spend more money to fix.

There are many more stories of so many billionaires or rich people who had been fighting to gain more money and ended up buying their health with their wealth. Some of them got cancer, and some ended up getting a stroke.

The key is that we don't always have to buy our wealth by sacrificing our health. Most of the time, our health issues came up because we did not intentionally take care of ourselves and did not enjoy the process; instead, we focused too much on achieving our final goals. If we only keep doing things and do not think about why we do it and what consequences if we do it. We will always face lots of unexpected tragedies or bad lucks in life. *Because we did not lead our life, and we let our life lead us.*

The stress of waiting kills the chance for us to enjoy ourselves when we want so badly to achieve the final goal but are still in the process. To enjoy the process is to learn how to enjoy the failure, setbacks, and waiting time and keep believing that something good will happen every time and every day.

It is silly to say: "enjoy the failure, setbacks, and waiting time." right?

How? What do you mean? Let me share how I started my business and how I could enjoy it.

A bit of background here: I dreamed of bringing a logistics superhero HQ and started my company Signature Global Network. It's a global logistics network. I have almost 20 years of working experience in the logistics industry and 10 + years of network attendance experience, but I don't have any experience running a network. I started it based on my faith. Faith is something that you cannot see but still believe.

Long story short, I started it as I am always an actioner, but the process was complicated. You can imagine it as a fresh starter, and you must do everything yourself. Registration, accountant, administration, IT, Website, Marketing, Sales, etc. Trust me; I was passionate and excited. I had prepared for setbacks, difficulties, and challenges because I knew I would learn many things.

One day, I was so pumped by the problems with the guy who did my website at the beginning. It finally drove me crazy one day and did not affect my whole mood. My poor family became the victims. I remember that one day I was sitting in the car with my happy family; we were supposed to spend a beautiful weekend together, but it was all ruined because of my emotion from work. I changed this guy, but the missed days I was supposed to spend a good time with my family could not come back.

Then I realized and started to remind myself: Enjoy the process rule. I began to say to myself: Every pain I am suffering now is to bring myself and the business to a better level. *Rather than being frustrated and angry with the situation, rather than ruining my life and emotion because of losing life balance, why don't I just trust the process and just stop my work when I am supposed to enjoy family time?* It's challenging to change my habit, but **I planned more and more on my calendar**. I began to set up **boundaries** in my schedule so that I would intentionally put some nights for my kids and family.

If you are a business owner or about to start a business, please remember to 'enjoy the process. Only when you 'enjoy the process' can you be wiser to plan your schedule and prioritize your program to the most important things.

I say to myself every day that if I lose my life or family, what is the point of keeping working? Because of that, I balance more and more my family and work time more. Because of that, I love more of my work more. I could perform 100% in different roles. There might be one slow or down day, but that is ok. The key is to 'enjoy the process so we can run the infinite game.

The third step: **Finish strong.**

How many people succeeded simply because they finished well? Many failed because they couldn't wait till the end and gave up. There is a common fallacy here that is called The Sunk Cost Fallacy. The sunk cost fallacy is a logical fallacy that entails sticking with a loss or failed venture because you've already invested a significant amount of time, money, or other resources that you can't get back. We know how important it is to finish strong, but how can we do it easier?

First, if we find the key to 'enjoying the process, it helps us to keep going in the long run because we do not feel like waiting as we are already on a happy journey. However, enjoying the process does not mean we can finish well unless we keep our 'honeymoon attitude.'

The common problem is that when we are new to something, we will have a honeymoon time. My key to finishing well is to keep my honeymoon attitude, which helps me to be passionate and 110% in everything. Including every relationship that I have.

Are you familiar with the stories about the honeymoon? A honeymoon married time. When both husband and wife were just like the actual prince and princess, saying sweet words about each other with 100% full respect. You know, no need to think about the future, and there seems to be only You and Me, the loving birds' life. It feels like nobody else exists and our life is just perfect. Why? Why can we think like that when we are on honeymoon time? Why can't we bring that feeling to an end?

How about a honeymoon work time? When you start a new job, you are excited and can't stop doing more. You just wanted to ask more questions, do the best you could, and get to know everybody. Do you just feel that you are so unique and full of new things and ideas? Even though you make a mistake or ask silly questions, you are not afraid because you are on your honeymoon with the company. People just forgive you quickly, and you just show lots of respect for each other. But why can't this last to the end?

Suppose you want to become a natural leader in people's lives and finish well. You must keep the 'Honeymoon Attitude.' What I mean by that attitude isn't to encourage you to make more mistakes; it is to take action to make an effort just like the first time you start it. It applies to everything you do and every relationship you run.

Why do so many relationships become less heated, but only a few are heated more? The funny story in married life was when a couple got married for a month or a year. The story was when the wife said: "Honey, can you help to bring the bin out?" Then the husband will go straight away without even thinking. They would appreciate each other and not take anything offensive. Then here comes the version after maybe three months or one year. Wife: "Bin." Husband: "Why don't you bring it? Why is it my turn again?" All conversations start to become aggressive and completely different. What's changed? **The attitude.**

See if the wife could maintain a honeymoon attitude; she could probably say things nicely and appreciate more. If the husband could maintain a honeymoon attitude, he could do it without complaining. Everything takes two sides, but one side must make an effort first. Either side. Will you be the leader in making an effort?

Back to my work attitude, I have been a leader and managed many teams. Still, I always keep my honeymoon attitude, never forgetting how I started, which helps me remain humble and more respectful to others. It also helped me to get closer to people in any department. Sometimes in the logistics industry, like many other office environments, you may see lots of politics. Some people may feel that they are higher or more senior than you, so they may look down upon you or don't respect you. I saw many cases like that. But it didn't shake my determination to be the one who keeps my honeymoon attitude to keep learning and growing. Keep respecting and being open to helping more people and learning new things. No matter if you are a professor or a teacher. A president or a prime minister. Every one of us has limited knowledge, and everyone should have something that we can learn.

If you want to finish well, always keep the 'honeymoon attitude' when you first married in the honeymoon time, the attitude when you first started your job. That hunger for growing, being respectful, and being humble is the most significant gift and tool to help you finish well.

You have unlocked the secrets of your leadership self-empowerment. The last chapter is to get you ready and have yourself running a leadership mindset that will always get you back on track to transformation. You will never get lost and always find your way back when facing new challenges. You will find the keys to staying motivated all the time.

CHAPTER EIGHT

Joyful self-motivated leadership.

Lead your best life.

*T*ime to activate your self-motivated power now. I am much more self-controlled, resilient, and patient in a leadership role in the corporate world. When I removed that hat from me, I lost my good habits. Then I realize I am the one who decides if I remove my cap or not, and I determine what roles and hats I choose to wear today in my life. Why should I remove it if it does good for me?

Are you ready to activate your power and keep that unstoppable power in you? Let's start with unlocking your inner sparkle. *Choose to be the star in real life.*

So many of us have dreamed of being superstars, but not many of us remember that we can be one in our real life, not fictional life. *The good part of being a star isn't because you are a star but because you shine and bring light and sparkle to others.*

We have unlocked our self-empowerment; now it is time for us to unlock more leadership in you for you to shine and spread our sparkle!

Because only making a difference and growing could help us manifest our unshakable happiness in life.

How many of us want to make a difference, and how many want to be superstars? We were born desiring to be a leader and to shine, as we know it will bring us joy. Do you know that a leader is a star? Can a star be a leader? If you become well-known, people follow you because you lead the trend. Being a star in our life is more beneficial and authentic.

I had my time, too, the time chasing my dreams to become a famous superstar like many of you. Here is my story.

When I was 19, I finished the TV show one day and got a great experience on the show, but it also made me feel down once the show ended. My life is back to a routine and dull lifestyle. Then there's an inner voice coming up to me and saying: do you want to be a famous star? Be recognized in real life, be the star in real life. It was like an awakening call to me. I found my way and purpose to live daily to show people kindness and love. I helped people in the office a lot. I showed respect and always smiled at people, regardless of whether they were in a high or a low position. I was always full of energy and passion for whatever I did. I believe that I am a star in real life. A star is supposed to shine in other people's life. A celebrity makes a difference. I believed it so much and became a star whenever I went. I found my inner sparkle.

That didn't just make me feel so good, I found my personality started to attract people from everywhere who wanted to be close to me and enjoy the sparkle I spread. I got compliments from many people in the office saying: You are like a star! Then I laughed and would say to them: Yes, I am. I enjoy being a star in real life; in other words, I decided to be a leader, and I believe I was born to be a leader.

I chose to be the star in real life and make a difference. Don't worry that nobody will like you for those who haven't got any dates or partners yet. Just choose to be the leader of your sparkle and focus on being a star in real life to make a difference. You will meet your Mr. or Mrs. and be at the best time when you focus on getting yourself to the best version of every day.

Be the star in real life that lights up hope in someone's life! The lead shows them that in this life, there are good things and good people they can believe in, the star shines every day, but you don't even realize how many lives are positively impacted by you! Not because you don't want to know but because you are so busy shining and lighting others that change many people's lives to more remarkable places.

Before you can find your sparkle and be the star of other people's lives, you need to understand that a successful leader has the duty and responsibility to do regular self-checks if you want to improve yourself to a better version every day! Only then can you find more of your sparkle.

I loved to be the sparkle, even though it was just how I lived my life. I would hear good words from people: "Wow, you are like a sparkle!' 'Wow, you are so powerful!' "Wow, you are so inspirational!' To hear these isn't about how good I am but about knowing how much difference I could bring. The best thing about being a leader and a sparkle in people's lives is that we know life is tough, and it needs more sparkles to remind us how good life could be if we change our perspective and choose to lead our thoughts to be the leader of ourselves.

Here are three big things I learned about leadership from my life experience:

- First, **Leadership is a skill that anybody could be trained to have**

I always believe I was born a leader because I have been a leader since primary school and even until today. But I truly believe that leadership is a skill everybody could be trained to have.

- Second, **leadership is a choice**

Everybody has the right to choose to be a leader because someone could be born with a leadership personality but never be successful because they don't use their skills or practice them intentionally. If you don't consciously decide to be a leader, the skills can disappear as time passes.

- Thirdly, **being a leader is like being a Mum or Dad**

These are the elements that I find I have in my leadership life: Responsibility/Influencer/Parenting.

But I do have questions for you:

Do you want to be a leader, and do you decide to do so?
I ask because if you don't want to do something and end up doing it, you will end up miserable. Because what you do is against your will unless you decide you are determined to do it. Only when we choose to do something can we then make commitments. So yes, when you decide to be a leader, you are responsible for doing what leaders need to do.

Do you only want to enjoy the good part of being a leader, not the hard part?
It is very much like being a parent. We all hear stories about how hard it is to give birth, but why are so many women willing to do it? Because we all know that only by going through the pain can we get a new life, and how amazing is that?

To be a leader isn't just to think of taking credit but also need to prepare for the hard part – responsibility.

It is just like you decide to raise a child if you don't like the process of raising them. When they get naughty, which every child will, we can't just send the child away. Probably every parent ever had that one-second wrong thought of putting the baby back into the tummy when the baby made them exhausted. The reality was that we couldn't, so we had to keep moving on and facing it.

When we decide to be a leader, we should commit to helping guide people in our team to be the best of themselves. *We cannot control their actions, but we can advise and influence them.*

'Being a leader makes me stronger every day and prepares me for more blessings and bigger things in life.'

I remember when I started being a manager, and I did not have anyone to train me or teach me how. I had to keep trying. There were days I made wrong decisions, but when I looked at my team, who looked up to me, my resilience and inner power immediately became more substantial. I realized that we can be much stronger than we ever think, particularly when we are holding strong with responsibility.

Here are the Five Golden Rules for your leadership mindset that activate your unstoppable leadership power.

Leadership Mindset Golden rule #1: The hidden beauty in your suffering.

It may sound terrible, but the ugly truth is that we only grow when we feel pain. Things we need to remember: If you want an easier life, do hard things, and if you want a hard life, do the easier things.

I always ask my daughter a question when she wants to give up. I would ask her do you choose a more challenging life in the future or if you're going to choose an easier life. She would answer me: easier life.

I: "Ok, if you climb a mountain, it will be challenging at the beginning, but what happens next? Is it easier to go up or come down?

My daughter: It will be much easier when we go down.

Yes, our life is like that. If we want to climb a mountain, we will see beautiful views and have to make lots of effort, but it will be rewarding. It will be easier later once we have trained to strengthen and get more ready to go down."

The mountain example also reminds me that sometimes, you do

not want to choose to be a leader or don't want to get ready. Then you will be hit more painfully if you choose to be reactive rather than proactive because **it is always easier to make an easy choice but wrong than to make a hard choice but right**. Our life is always like a marathon with your time:

> If you move forward, it will move forward for you; You make small efforts each day, and you are still going ahead; But when you stop moving, your time won't wait, which means you are going backward.

How many people are only successful because they have suffered so much pain? Every one of us suffers pain in life, but if we are like most of us, avoid the pain, hate, and complain about it. We will never see the hidden beauty and achieve our final goals. Ordinary people turn pains into scars, and extraordinary people turn pains into strength.

Find the hidden beauty of every pain that comes up in your life. When you feel the most challenging time is now in front of you, and you seem unable to deal with it, believe that nothing will be worse and good things are coming your way. Only when you are willing to see its beauty and use your painful experiences can you truly turn it into strength.

Maybe it was your childhood suffering from domestic violence. Your story needs to be known because it will help many people like you to re-live a better life. Maybe it was your self-doubt story or committing suicide thought that almost took your life. You can be shameless and fearless to tell the world now that you have led your own life and live the best version of yourself. If you can, so can they.

Maybe it's a broken relationship you had with someone before that made you doubt yourself for a long time; then it is time for you to believe that you are enough and you are beautiful, because who you are is not what others decide for you. Choose your skim milk and be bold to live the 100% of your own version.

Leadership Mindset Golden rule #2- Everybody can be trained to be a leader if they choose to.

Are you a leader? Are you born or not born as a leader? There are answers to what you may have heard about the answers to the above questions:

- Someone was born a leader, but someone wasn't.
- Someone was chosen to be a leader, but someone wasn't.
- Leadership is a skill that everybody can learn. But here is what I concluded:
- You are all chosen to be a leader to lead your own life;
- Everyone can learn leadership skills.

When I say this, you may ask, what does that mean? If everyone is a leader, where are the followers?

I was born into a very ordinary family, one of the millions which aren't unique, and none of my parents or grandparents were any successful leaders in the big society. My grandpa (mum's Dad) is a farmer, and my grandma (Mum's mum) is a housewife who had eight children, and only six survived due to the poor conditions back then. My grandpa (Dad's Dad) was learning at school until probably high school, and it was when the 'Cultural Revolution' started in China he was arrested because he wanted to learn more. My grandma (Dad's mum) only learned in primary school, and then nothing anymore. She just lived a simple and happy life. So, to conclude that none of them have made a massive impact in history, and if I would choose to believe that if I weren't chosen to be a leader, I would never have become who I am today.

I decided to believe in good things in myself, even though it may not be me yet. It will come as long as I keep seeking it. It turned out that I was right. I have been seeking ways to be a great leader in my life and career. I managed it very well. It wasn't perfect, but I have been improving every single day. I will keep finding new things to improve in different roles and ways, but I believe all leadership skills are trainable. Practice makes perfect.

If you can be a person to make decisions every day, you can be a leader;

If you can do kind things in someone's life, you make a difference, and you can be a leader;

If you are a teacher, coach, or mentor, you can be a leader;

If you are a parent, you can be a leader;

Even if you are a kid who lives the best life of your own, your shining light can make you a leader;

A leader is an influencer who takes the initiative and intends to make a difference.

A leader is a person who is willing to take responsibility and take care of themselves as well as the people around them.

Only one thing can stop you from being a leader: your belief. Your belief guides your choice. Choose to be a leader today, and it shows the giant step of your trust and faith.

Leadership Mindset Golden Rule #3: Dangers of being double-minded. Choose to be firm.

One common mistake that every leader will make is 'doubt,' the 'double-minded.' Let me quickly share with you some stories.

It was my first time riding a horse, and I went there because I wanted to fulfill my daughter's will. The horses we were riding were huge. I love animals, and my daughter and I thought they were cute. I felt nervous and excited as it was my first time, particularly when I had to sign the liability of agreement before riding, which meant that if I died from this, they wouldn't take any responsibility.

The instructor taught us how to lead the horse, which sounds straightforward. He taught us when to kick or pull in the directions, which needs to be hard and firm. It went well at the beginning, but suddenly, the horse stopped walking while everybody else kept going, and the instructor was riding the other horse in front of me, and I tried to ask for help. I tried to use the way the instructor told me to, to kick a bit, but then I doubted, so the horse noticed my double mind, and immediately, it didn't follow up my instructions.

I was questioning my decision because I wasn't confident. Anyway, the instructor had to come. I saw him pulling so hard on the rein that the horse immediately realized it was a firm instruction that it had to obey.

The instructor just said one thing:"You must be firm." He said the horse was taking advantage of me because it knew I was soft to it. I was lucky, and I didn't fall off the horse. My point here is that it is always so dangerous to be double-minded.

I went to learn to ski for the very first time in Falls Creek in Victoria. It is a very famous snow mountain with great ski coaches. I did the class. After the whole lesson, we found a common issue for everyone when we doubted ourselves, the ski gesture would go wrong, and our bodies would shake. There is a crucial point for us to learn how to ski, and the first step is to be firm. Be firm on your decision, and then you will find out if it is working or not working. Or it will bring more confusion, and it will take a very long time for us to learn one thing. The fascinating part is that kids learned faster because they didn't carry too many distractions to shake their decisions. When they decided to go, they just went. So after the lesson, most kids became experts, but most new-beginner adults were not graduating.

How about driving on the road? What will be the most dangerous thing to do when you need to overtake or when you want to find the gold chance to turn right or left? I found that the most challenging thing is when you want to overtake or turn, you are unsure, and you tried but doubted and then doubted again. It would make the other side so frustrated and confused, and it is hazardous because people wouldn't know what to do by knowing nothing about your final intentional decision.

Isn't this a familiar situation for many people in leadership life? Is it like a parent trying to teach his child when he gives out the rules? If he constantly changes the rules, it confuses the child, who could take advantage and then becomes disobedient to the parents simply because they are not clear about the firm rules. They are confused because sometimes you say no, but sometimes you say yes. Or maybe you are a parent, but you let others lead your children, such as their grandparents or your partner, but you all don't communicate and agree in one mind? Then the child would go to the other person to ask for something you don't say yes to.

It is the same that we have our 'mind' and 'unconscious mind' leading our life. If we don't align these two minds continuously, it brings many problems and dangers. Also, our mind needs to be made up. That's why we always ask people: Have you made up your mind? If we trust the thought in our mind without thinking, that is called the 'unconscious mind.'

In my leadership growth, I made many mistakes like everyone else too.

One of the biggest mistakes was being firm and changing my mind when making a decision.

I remember when I doubted if I was too young to lead a team, and when someone raised their opinions, I started to challenge myself and change my mind. My biggest mistake was when I began to doubt myself and my decision. I realized it is not the right decision that makes us strong leaders; the courage to believe and take responsibility makes us strong leaders. A strong leader can make many mistakes, but they will keep going and not doubt the future. A great leader has a firm mind that knows nobody is perfect but is courageous to keep making progress and is not afraid of making mistakes by taking responsibility.

Enough doubting!! Enough judging! Be firm. Keep believing and never quit!

Are you who people say you are? Or? Are you a person whom you believe you are? Do you look at your company and what others say or see you are? Or do you look at it as what you think it will be?

Do you know how much noise I heard when I decided to run my business? Noises like: 'Are you sure? Good luck with that!' 'It's the worst time to start a network business.' 'Too many of them; how can you be different?' Do you know when you are afraid of doing something hard, what will you do? You will choose to listen to the 'kind advice' which could 'help' you to find excuses, and once you find enough reasons, it will get enough to scare you and stop you from doing it.

Trust me, the cases I experienced with judgment were countless, but how did I adjust myself?

We are facing judgment from many companies or people because they DON'T KNOW us, and they judge us as a 'New Network' and a 'beginner.' They see you as one of their previous 'disappointment experiences' because 'they don't know; they choose not to believe in you and decide to doubt you and judge you. They thought you were one of them and thought you had no difference from them. When we approached people to want to make an excellent connection and understand each other's business, I could tell that so many people were feeling insecure. They felt like we were trying to get benefits and values from them, even though we wanted to look at what we could potentially help. Sometimes, even a network connection is excellent. It is not always about business. It is more about relationships. If we could manage relationships, we could manage the business.

Do you have the exact moment as a smaller or medium organization? Do you sometimes feel that other big guys are looking down upon you? Or do clients judge you because you are not as big as the competitors? But if you think more about it, is it really 'bigger' is 'better'?

The more, the merrier. Or is it more about 'Quality'? You don't have to prove to them because the truth will reveal itself over time. Your success and your work will tell the truth.

Let me ask you!!! Aren't all successful companies starting from 'New' and 'Beginning'? Weren't you started from zero for all your business too? Why do you judge a person or a company with what you see now? Why don't you listen to their vision and invest in the future?

When I am doing my business, I don't see it now, and I see its future. I choose not to see the barriers because I know walls come, and I can handle them. As long as there's a will, there is a way. Our vision and the 'why' behind it will lead us to the best places. People may laugh at me or feel my dream is a bit unrealistic. Like Forest Gump, keep running your dream, let them laugh, and let them ignore you.

100% of the successful person you see today had challenging stories in their life, and they had tough times, and they were like every one of us! But there are things among all of them in common! They BELIEVE, they DO, and they NEVER QUIT!!!!

We know we are playing an infinite game, and the game won't be over, and we will always stand up and get up and keep going and NEVER GIVE UP!!!!

To all business owners or starters!! To whoever is struggling, keep going!! You decide to be who you are! If you don't have many audiences, be your own audience because one day, everyone will come and watch your show. Because you are too busy to live in others' shows. Your show may start a bit late, but it is always running and never stops.

Be firm about what you are going to do and be confident in the decision you make. You always have a chance to learn and grow from it.

Leadership Mindset Golden Rule #4 – 6Ps to stay self-motivated all the time.
Being a leader as the head of the body, most of the time, you do not have

another authority you can go to and consult with. Sometimes, even if you feel lonely, you must keep moving on and find your way to keep going. You must avoid being purposeless, and then you will stay highly self-motivated. You may ask how on earth you can stay self-motivated all the time.

Let's talk about self-motivation quickly.

Whoever deals with a child will understand that when you ask them to do something, they don't usually want to do it if they don't know why. They don't want to be forced or instructed to do anything unless they understand and know that it is good for them. Or they know the terrible consequence if they don't. Self-motivation is a thousand times better than 100 repeated reminders or enforcement.

When you are told to do something, your self-motivation will be low. Let me give you an example: one morning, as usual, I went to my daughter Sze Sze's room and woke her up.

Here are our conversations:

Version one:

> Me: "Hi, Sze Sze. Get up, brush your teeth, wash your face, then come for breakfast."
> Sze Sze: "Stop it, mum. I am tired. I don't want to get up." Still lying down and rolling around.

Then it could last forever, but she couldn't get any motivation to get up. There was another morning- version two:

> Me: "Sze Sze, we are going to the Royal Melbourne show! Do you want to go earlier?"
> Sze Sze: "Yeah!" Got up within 1 minute and got dressed up and ready in 5 minutes, with no complaints or drama.

The more evident difference between our conversations was that Sze Sze felt I was leading and trying to control her in the first conversation. She thought it was not her decision to get up, but I forced her. Her motivation was super low, and she even wanted to do things against my advice.

But the second conversation gave her the responsibility of leading her own time and behaviour. It creates high motivation because her own will leads her to the action.

Each of us is similar to my daughter. When our self-motivation is low when we don't think we are the leaders of the decisions. If we do what we are told, it is usually not 100% unless we determine it by ourselves; but if we are the decision-makers, we will put in 100% effort. How funny is that? It's the same person doing the same thing. But with a different initiative, the outcome will be so much different. When you are not choosing to be proactive, you are reactive.

So, to stay self-motivated, the key is to constantly and intentionally act as leaders of our own decisions and be courageous to take responsibility. Prepare for the worst, but wish for the best.

The good news is that I have concluded the answers to the 6 Ps.

Purpose

A life without purpose won't take you very far. Living a purpose-driven life is essential.

A widespread example for whoever has primary or younger kids at home, you will find the fascinating fact that during school days, the kids are always unwilling to get up from their beds and go to school. Still, surprisingly, during school holidays, they become their alarms. Sze Sze could wake up at 4-5 am when she went to her friend's house for a sleepover. It shows us that 'nothing is impossible to a willing heart.' The question is, where will you find your will? The will is the purpose.

It would be best if you found purpose in everything you do. If you do something just for the sake of doing it, it will burn your motivational bridge. To keep your motivation, you must find purpose regularly in the long and short term.

Ask yourself what and why. Don't worry about how. Because once you figure out what and why you will find out how automatically.

Passion

When you find your purpose, you will find your passion. You will lose your passion if you do something without a purpose. To do something you love is called passion; to do something you hate is called stress. To stay motivated, you must find your passion for everything you choose to do.

Passion brings joy, and a good relationship needs passion too. Passion brings a bonding connection to your relationship.

Working in one industry for about 20 years, how could I always stay in my passionate zone? Married to one man for almost 13 years, how could I always remain loving and heating up?

First, I am like all of you; there were always days I felt down, and my passion seemed to fade away, and I would allow myself to stay in a quiet and calm zone for a bit. But when I have been in a comfort zone or unchanged status for too long, I will start to think about the purpose of what I am doing, and I will begin to do new things and accept new challenges. I will have to keep raising my standard for a unique purpose again. If not, I will start to feel frustrated or unhappy.

For example, when I have been in a calm zone, which I thought was a quiet zone, I would later realize it was a purposeless zone. When we lose passion and stay in the calm zone, it is no longer a healthy zone. It is a dangerous and meaningless calm zone that will take our joy away. Because what I found is that only when I make progress and keep growing can make me happy, which was mentioned in the previous chapters.

Feeling down in a calm zone is like not feeling very happy or miserable. I started to hide many of my emotions and try to avoid them, and I thought this could bring me peace. If you want peace, you avoid talking to people and living in a box alone, which is unhealthy and does not bring a sense of long-lasting peace.

Then I finally realized that an immense sparkle in me is my passion! Only having a purposeful passion can bring me true peace and joy. It is so obvious if I don't bring my passion with me when I meet someone, my conversation will become less exciting and with less effort to this conversation. I couldn't light up the room.

But if I bring my passion, I get sparkle whenever I go. A good example is that since I was only 18, I travelled overseas and attended many international meetings with people I had never met. I had two choices when I met them. The first choice is to say hi and say things and then let fate decide if we will remember each other and if they would consider giving business to our company. Or I had the other choice, to cherish that moment to know one more friend. Yes, I didn't realize that my purpose was to know everyone honestly, listen to their stories with a genuine heart, and make more and more friends. So, it worked. My passion comes from my purpose: Loving people and connecting with people. It is one of the best things I could have, and I still carry it wherever I go. My sparkle comes from my passion for people and my purpose to know them personally.

The other story keeps my passion with a great purpose:

> COVID lockdown hit many people, especially people in Melbourne. Melbourne has been one of the most liveable cities in the world and just became the most extended lockdown city in a short time.
>
> I had been doing well in my routine, and I kept my passion well because every day, I would dress up like going to the office

with my make-up done even though I was always staying home. I was always ready for any client meetings or online meetings. I didn't even wear shorts or PJs anytime, even though I knew people would not see anything below my tummy in a camera.

My reason is simple: I always believe that opportunity would only go to those well prepared. I am always ready for any chance and anything that is coming up in my way. I wear professionally, and my make-up could bring me confidence because I know I am leading my life, and I decided to get ready at any time. In the meantime, when I started to talk to colleagues around, I realized that those who wear PJs had to keep cameras off, or they had to spend time changing, or they would miss critical things, and they were not able to lead their life, but instead, life is leading them.

There is no judgment because life is a choice, but if you want to lead your life and passion, always get ready!

Plan
What is your life attitude? There are different types of choices we have amongst all of us.

> A: I plan, and I do.
> B: I plan, but I don't do all of them on the list.
> C: I don't plan, but I do.
> D: I don't plan, so I don't do much.

Suppose your answer is A. Congratulations because 100% of successful people will plan. I used to be B, C, and D type in the different seasons.

What is essential to know is that if you don't plan your life, your time will fly, and you won't get much done.

People always ask me how I can do so many things simultaneously.

How can you be a mum, a wife, a business owner, or an author but still do volunteer work? How can you maintain your life balance with so many things going on? Because I plan.

To keep yourself motivated, you must plan things. Regularly plan your schedule even though you know you may change a bit of the plan on the actual situation. But if you don't plan things, you will be preparing for unexpected problems, losing track, and losing motivation, too, because you will get stuck and become reactive to what will happen next.

Keeping regular plans on your journal or mobile calendars is super important. Sometimes I realize that I have done everything on my plan list simply because I have marked them down and intentionally checked what I have done or haven't. However, I also tried days that my plan list is empty; I could have plenty of things undone, then I feel less motivated to do it, and I may leave these things to unknown dates.

Deadline.
To plan things, you must put down the deadline for each item. The timeline must be strict but with a specific boundary. For example, if I don't put a timeframe on things I need to do, that thing can sit there for a while, then you will get used to it sitting there. So, I always plan things weekly and daily with a clear timeline and deadlines.

Be Specific.
With the daily ones, I have a list of specific times with specific items too. If my plan for the day as working is 'Working,' I will never have much work done, and I probably will be distracted by simply checking a few emails and waiting for things to come my way, and my day will be very unproductive. My habit is to write down a clear to-do list with specific items. The more detailed, the better. Sometimes I have 20 items in a day, but I can at least tick many of them so that the pending ones can go to the next day.

If my plan is too broad such as spending time with family, when it is time for me to spend time with family, I may be distracted by something else and assume that if I am with my kids around, I am already spending time with them. So, to make my plan more practical, I will have to break them down into things like reading with my little one; Telling a story to my daughter; Dancing together, and so on.

Allow boundary.
To have boundaries is that you will have to understand no matter how many things you have planned, things can always go the other way because of unexpected things. It doesn't mean you always change your plan with excuses.

For example, when I suddenly planned one day with complete activities and productive work, I suddenly received a call from the school. I must pick up my daughter and send her to the emergency or stuff like that, I knew things would be different from what I had planned, but it's ok because that's life. So, I had to adjust myself quickly and adjust the plan. Keep the same goals, but promptly swap strategies and priorities today with another day. Therefore, it is essential to leave at least one day a week with fewer plans and some rest and spiritual recharge. I would suggest reading and studying the bible. It is the best book in the world, with everything you need to give you a peaceful mind.

It is ok if some days things happen. Trusts me, it won't be every day. At least in my life, 90% of the time, I have done everything on my list without interruptions or unexpected situations. When the 10% interruptive days come, I would treat it as my adventure day, bringing me super peace.

Enjoy planning!
Enjoy planning is critical. Because if you feel you are forced to, you will not have a great plan done for yourself.

Imagine a day with no plan, you finish your day, but you feel no fulfillment or achievement. You think that something is missing. No satisfaction, no joy. Instead, you have something or everything ticked from your to-do list on a day with plans. It feels so good with a peaceful mind, and your heart is full of joy because you have gained fulfillment. You don't have time to overthink or complain because you have so many meaningful things to do on the list. You keep your focus on the core things in life with plans too. Without goals, you can easily wander around and lose your purpose because you will hand your leadership to your time, not take the lead of your own time.

If you calculate how many days you still have left on earth based on a human's average age of 80 years or even up to 100 years, you will understand 'life is too short not to enjoy.' If you are 30 years old now, you only have 18,250 days to live; if you are 50 years old, you only have 10,950 days. And if you are 80 now, congratulations; every day is a blessing and a gift.

Now you have a choice. Let your life take you and waste your last days on earth or take your lead and plan your days and trips. Do as many meaningful things as possible for the rest of your life.

I love planning and treat it as one of the best times. Whenever I plan, I have a fresh mind and bring new ideas. It is time for me to conclude and learn. The more I do it, the more I will understand myself and make the best plans for myself.

I love planning because it helps me live the best life I could have managed. I know that sometimes change and unexpected things will come my way to ruin my plan. But it allows me to adjust my expectations and include these surprising things in my schedule.

I love it because every time I spend 20 minutes planning, it helps my 4 hours of work become much more effective. If I start doing things without guidance or direction, my day can finish with only a few things done and with no surprise. But If I have planned, the excellent outcome isn't that I have done much more than I expected, but also that I do it much better by knowing why I needed to do it.

Try it and do it at least once a week for one month, then another month. Once you get to 21 days or more, it will become part of you, and you will miss that. Do it on a Sunday night because the week starts. That's what I do.

Do a yearly, monthly, weekly, and daily plan.

You will get huge rewards and return if you try it. And remember to plan is the best time to lead your time and your life. A plan helps you to learn and grow from your previous experiences. Once you understand why you do the plan, the more you try, the more you will love to do it.

Pledge

To pledge is to commit. To do things without commitment is just a waste of time. If we decide to do something, we must commit to it. What is your pledge for your life commitments? Pledge what you need to do to keep motivated.

Only when you know there's no way back can you find more ways forward. A pledge is also a Promise. I learned a significant thing when I was little. I understand that 'never promise unless you can deliver.' So, to pledge means, you are committed to doing something.

Pledge isn't just for the time when you become a citizen of that country. It is a life attitude and leadership attitude that you commit your responsibility to yourself and your own life. If doing everything has nothing to do with 'pledging,' you will always find excuses instead of responsibilities.

One of the beneficial things that I have been using in my life is the 'pledge attitude' to my roles. I may not be as perfect, but whenever I determine something, I pledge to do it as 110% as I can.

In my previous workplace, people were always surprised that what I did wasn't just to do my work but also to make a difference, and they could see my determination and 'going the extra mile attitude. I do it because I pledge to be a leader in my own life; alternatively, it impacts and inspires others.

Persistence

When you pledge to do something, it takes more than once or sometimes even hundreds of times to reach the bigger or the most meaningful goals. Persistence is the key to making things happen, especially for the hard stuff.

The difference between a successful guy and an unsuccessful one is that the first will keep doing until the end. Still, the second one won't last until the end, as persistence needs patience, which is one of the biggest challenges to all human beings.

All the Olympic athletes will be able to do what they are doing if they give up. If you do one thing once, will a miracle come to you? When you say someone is so lucky, but in most cases, they are so hard-working and persistent. Their willingness to repeat one thing hundreds of times and thousands of times makes the difference.

If you want to do anything, spend more time on it and let it be persistent, you will become an expert. Someone says that if you spend five years learning and doing one thing, you will become an expert.

Persistence isn't easy because it can be boring sometimes when you have been doing something for a while, but the excellent time seems never to come. Therefore, we need the patience to help with our persistence.

Patience

We live in a fast food, knowledge, and delivery world. We don't even need to go out, and we can watch movies on TV. We don't need to queue, and the food or products we purchase will be delivered through online orders. But **let's be genuine: worthwhile things take time.** Let's give ourselves time to achieve better things.

Yes, patience is vital. Without patience, we won't be joyful and will lose many golden opportunities. Do you think the smartphone we have today was invented in one day and with one experiment? No, it started with a telephone and a giant computer. Do you think the vacuum we have today was invented all at once? No, it started with a broom. Many new generations don't see brooms anymore, but that's part of the success.

It is so easy to say be patient, but it is one of the hardest things in the world for human beings. Funnily, according to one of my friend's sons, "Patience is the most boring thing in the world." We don't like it, but it is so essential. There are so many things we know are correct that will help us, but we couldn't handle them very well. But let's keep trying, and practice makes perfect.

You may be familiar with the cars on the road, and you let it go when one car tried to overtake you. However, after 1 or 2 minutes, you find yourself ahead of that car by doing your speed. See, this is the point I want to make. Sometimes, even if we are in a rush and impatient, it doesn't improve our results. Instead, it ruined our peace and made us anxious.

Be patient until you have more credits, and then you can find the best opportunity to speak to your boss about your expectations for a salary increase or any demand you have.

Be patient with growing and learning to where you want to be, just like the seed sitting under the ground for a long time that you couldn't even notice, until one day it just grows up again and again into a big tree and produces so many fruits.

Keeping patients is aligned with our faith and trust. If we believe and trust that things will come, it gives us more capacity to be patient.

The other thing we need to do is to turn our focus on things to do while waiting rather than purely waiting. If you see that popular restaurant with a long queue, how are these people willing to wait for so long? Are they just standing there doing nothing? If that's the case, the line will soon disappear as I will be so surprised if there are so many patients waiting unless they are waiting for billions of dollars or a free bonus. In most cases, these people could keep waiting for something that keeps them busy chatting with a friend or checking and playing on their smartphones.

The 'Haidilao hotpot' business was founded in 1994 in Sichuan, China, but it suddenly became so hot and popular in China. When I returned to visit China in 2018, it grew crazily well-known everywhere. A friend told me from Singapore that the owner in Singapore became the richest person since then until COVID hit. One of the biggest and most different things they do is provide free services to all customers while waiting. They helped you watch younger kids and provided free nail polish service. Do you know how attractive a 'free lunch' is to people?

Patience is a magical key to keeping you motivated; you need to find a way to keep yourself patient. The outcome will always come if you keep doing what you do and focusing.

Leadership Mindset Golden Rule #5 Be a decision-maker. – Intentionally make your decisions today.

Remember the 'skim milk please moment?'

When you don't intentionally choose to make a decision, a decision will be made for you.

When you don't seize an opportunity, an opportunity will be taken by others.

When you don't intentionally choose to deal with your life, your life will deal with you.

When you don't intentionally choose to do something you love, something you don't love will choose you.

When you don't intentionally fill your mind with positive things, bad and negative things will fill your mind.

When you don't intentionally choose to work on your joy, your joy will walk away.

When you don't intentionally choose to lead your life, your life will be led by others.

Say to yourself today:

I decided to be the light!
I decided to be extraordinary.
I decided to be a good leader who leads my thoughts and decisions!
I decided to be the one who would light up my inner leadership power completely.
I decided to be happy, joyful, and peaceful.
I decided to admit that everyone has at least one last choice even when everything is against me, and I feel like 'no choice anymore.' That is: I decide to respond differently.

Be a decision-maker in your own life, be a leader in your own life, be an extraordinary leader, and be the best version of yourself by intentionally making wise decisions and choices. Be a warrior defending your world with joy, peace, faith, and love.

It's never easy to decide on life because it's never possible for us to delight everyone.

If you make a choice, expect noises.
If you make a choice, expect hardships.
If you make a choice, expect objections.
But… …
If you choose this way, never regret it!
If you choose this way, never be afraid!
If you choose this way, never give up!
Unless you tried, and then you have to choose again.
But if you don't do it or try it, how do you know it's not working?

Never be afraid to make decisions!

Never too late to make a change after trying. It may look bad to change, admit mistakes, or put down our pride.

But... ...

Always remember that we don't do the easy things; we do the right things.

Sometimes, it might be too hard for you initially, but remember that only hard times create strong people! Easy times create weaker people! So, to be extraordinary, you need to do hard things, which will lead you to a better path.

Keep practicing, and your powerful little magic will start to change your inner world, your small world, and the whole world – the people around you.

Last but not least, you are either leading or being led. Be confident and firm about your decisions. Keep learning and never stop loving. As time goes by, your wisdom will only grow more, not less. Enjoy your joyful leadership in your life. You are meant to make an impact on this world.

Life is like a mirror; you smile, it smiles; You frown, it frowns. Life is also like taking a photo; the way and direction how you choose to click the button leading the final result; Good Attitude changes your life! The choices are yours!

You are much stronger than you ever think or know! Now it's time for you to ride your joyful leadership journey!

Bonus Powerful Quotes

I love writing my reflections all the time. Whenever some life experience and powerful words come to my mind, I want to write them down and be empowered and reminded.

These words are inspired by my life experiences and messages I have read or heard but come initially from my thoughts and conclusions.

I love how small and simple things have so much power in us if we can understand and apply them to our lives.

These 52 Powerful Quotes Every Week throughout a year for you to read and remember and to be reminded, You Will See an Amazing Transformation in Life!

What can you do with these quotes?

- Write them down somewhere in your room/fridge/Notebooks or anywhere you can hardly not see.
- Check it every morning when you wake up and before sleep every night.
- Use it when you are feeling stuck or down.

1. A leader is also an ordinary person, but his courage and will to make decisions and take responsibilities set them away from the ordinary and make them extraordinary.
2. Leadership starts with leading yourself.
3. Your Life is a leadership choice, and you are the decision-maker.

4. A good choice can change your Life, but you must start with making one.
5. A leader is an influencer, and every one of us has been an influencer in different areas.
6. Your Life is a movie, and you are the movie director. Stop living in other people's movies and be the insignificant cast.
7. Two attitudes in Life, which one will you choose?
   You try, you fall, you doubt, and you fail.
   You try, you fall, you believe, you stand up, you believe, you try again, and again and again, you succeed.
8. Whenever you feel stuck in Life, don't overthink; find your' Goal (Purpose)' and 'Faith (Belief)' to move on.
9. We don't do what's easier or makes us feel better; we do what's right because that will make us better.
10. You are unique and beautiful and the most qualified candidate to represent yourself. – Love yourself.
11. Outside beauty fades with time, but inner beauty increases when you grow wiser.
12. The joyful leader in you is your hidden treasure.
13. Our youth will decrease, but our experience and strength will increase.
14. To love is a choice you lead; loving others isn't purely about helping others; it's also about helping yourself.
15. Through loving others, we become more powerful and whole.
16. "Love" is a verb, not a noun; it needs actions with effort.
17. Love action brings more fruits in love relationships.
18. Only leaders who love themselves could have the capability to love their followers.
19. Despite our skin/eye/hair colours, we are all human beings and beautiful in different ways; Rare is precious; if we all look the same, it will be dull and no more precious.

20. Being offensive is a choice, and a joyful leader will avoid that choice.
21. Changing is not a choice, and it's happening every day, but we choose to change for better or worse.
22. Joy brings long-term happiness, and being grateful brings joy.
23. A truly successful leader leads with a joyful heart.
24. A true leader doesn't need a title to be a leader; their followers are their title.
25. Letting go doesn't mean completely forgetting; it is a choice to remember it, but with no more aches or pain because you have chosen to forgive both people and things that hurt you.
26. Your past is a good teacher but a lousy leader.
27. Life contains good and bad, but without either side, the other won't exist; However, the wise choose to focus on the good.
28. To build up muscles is hard and painful, but it is good for you; To forgive others is hard and painful, but it is good for you.
29. A leader moves on fast with offenses or mistreatment because they know that dwelling on the past is a waste of time.
30. Fear can stop you from making significant decisions and extraordinary things.
31. Switch off your false alarm fear mechanisms.
32. Only Faith can drive away your fears; find your Faith today.
33. Being faithful doesn't mean that you will never be worried or fearful again; it just means that no matter what is lying ahead, you will not be afraid, and you will get there.
34. What you believe will happen in your Life; so, think for good.
35. Always believe in the good of people because the words ' I believe in you ' is powerful.
36. The trouble and setbacks will always be there, but your strong belief will always show you the way to reach your good goals.
37. Being a leader doesn't mean that you need to know everything; it means you are courageous to take the lead and responsibilities.

38. Speaking powerfully to yourself will strengthen your thoughts and lead you to decisive actions.
39. When you have a great goal, think about the purpose carefully, start it quickly, enjoy the process slowly, and finish the ending strongly.
40. it is always easier to make an easy choice but wrong than to make a hard choice but right.
41. If we never give up, there will never be a finishing line to define who is the winner.
42. When you don't seize an opportunity, an opportunity will be taken by others.
43. When you don't intentionally choose to lead your Life, your Life will be led by others and be out of your blueprints.
44. Committing to being a leader gives you more responsibilities, resilience, and strength to do Life; it shuts down excuses and makes you less vulnerable but more joyful.
45. "Being Vulnerable" is a choice; It is popular nowadays, but we should focus on awareness and acknowledgment, not misuse it for excuses to get ourselves out of that 'vulnerable trap.'
46. A wise leader listens for listening rather than for responding.
47. Creating a good habit will need high self-discipline and commitment, and the best way is to add that into your daily routine, just like 'sleeping, eating, and drinking.' Because if you allow any excuse not to do it, it will be harder for you to build it up again.
48. Only when you find your purpose more significant than yourself can you find true happiness.
49. Your purpose stimulates your Faith, and your Faith will lead you to achieve your goals (purpose).
50. Focus on the cores, and you shall consistently achieve more!
51. Expect noises when you decide to do something because nobody will delight everyone, and a good decision can still upset someone.

52. Being smart but arrogant = foolish
    Being smart but humble = wise

    Being knowledgeable but proud = foolish
    Being knowledgeable but humble = wise

    Being rich but selfish = foolish
    Being rich but kind = wise

    Last but not least: Always be humble and always spread kindness.

It's time to celebrate!

Request Your Free **The extra 52 life-changing quotes**. & Join a free Joyful Leaders Academy Facebook Community so that you can get first-hand information, VIP discounts for her future books, coaching and business programs.

As a way of saying thank you for purchasing a copy of my book, I am gifting you a free copy of the bonus of The Extra 52 Life-Changing Quotes that is exclusive to readers of The Joyful Leader In You.

Claim your free copy and space on The Joyful Leaders Academy by emailing to: sgninfo@signaturegln.com

Follow Kristy on her social channels:
LinkedIn: https://www.linkedin.com/in/cuilan-kristy-guo-1776b5182
Instagram: Kristy_guochangemaker
Facebook public main page: https://www.facebook.com/kristyguochangemaker/
Twitter: @Cuilanguo

www.ingramcontent.com/pod-product-compliance
Lightning Source LLC
Chambersburg PA
CBHW070253010526
44107CB00056B/2441